I0397227

The Advanced Forex and Options Trading Guide

Learn The Vital Basics & Secret Strategies For Day Trading in The Forex & Options Market! Make Your Online Income Today by Becoming a Top Trader!

By Neil Sharp

"The Advanced Forex and Options Trading Guide: Learn The Vital Basics & Secret Strategies For Day Trading in The Forex & Options Market! Make Your Online Income Today by Becoming a Top Trader!" Written by "Neil Sharp".

The Advanced Forex and Options Trading Guide is a bundle of the books "The Advanced Options Trading Guide", & "The Advanced Forex Trading Guide".

Hope You Enjoy!

The Advanced Options Trading Guide

The Best Complete Guide for Earning Income with Options Trading, Learn Secret Investment Strategies for Investing in Stocks, Futures, ETF, Options, and Binaries.

By Neil Sharp

Table of Contents

Introduction

Thank you for purchasing *The Advanced Options Trading Guide. The Best Complete Guide for Earning Income with Options Trading, Learn Secret Investment Strategies for Investing in Stocks, Futures, ETF, Options, and Binaries.* I am sure that this book will live up to your expectations.

If you have purchased this book, it is because you are interested in learning more about options trading and how this type of trading can help you make a profit as a result of your investment activities.

As you will see in the following pages, this book contains a wealth of information that you will not find readily available anywhere else. In fact, many of the concepts found in this book are not easily found in a single volume. Often, you would have to consult numerous sources in order to find all of this information in a single source.

You will also find that options trading is an extensive topic. But fear not, we will go step by step in such a way that grasping these concepts will not be as hard as you think. If you happen to have prior knowledge with some understanding of this topic, then I am sure that you will find a clear understanding of the options trading markets. If you are already familiar with this topic, then I hope that you will find new information that will help you expand your current knowledge and gain a fresh perspective on this matter.

Options trading differs somewhat from regular equities trading. With equities, you were dealing with publicly traded companies. Of course, the options market also deals with publicly traded companies but the difference lies in that options are considered part of the derivatives market. As such, the derivatives market is far larger and far more complicated than the traditional equities market.

Consequently, it will certainly help you to learn more about how the derivatives market works, especially since there are many opportunities available for investors in derivatives. So don't be intimidated by the vast amount of information available out there with reference to the derivatives market. In reading this book, I hope that you get a clear idea of how the derivatives market, through options trading, can open up newer opportunities for investors such as yourself.

For most professional investors, options are a common tool that is used to help protect themselves from volatile markets and sudden swings in the prices of equities and commodities. This is why it is important to also understand the nature of equities and commodities.

Since options are considered derivatives, you are not exactly trading an equity or commodity, that is, a specific security that is attached to the contract which you are negotiating. That's being said, it is vital to have a clear perspective on the dynamics of each market.

Each of the chapters in this book is dedicated to illustrating how each of these markets interacts in such a way that a broader structure is revealed as part of the global structure of financial markets.

The good thing about all of this is that highly technical knowledge is not required. All you need is some time and dedication in order for you to gain a considerable grasp of the concepts discussed throughout this book.

So buckle up because we are going to drill down into the concepts which make up the options trading markets and thereby broader financial markets, not just in the United States, but also around the world. Bear in mind the teas are global markets we are talking about. So keeping an open mind and the global perspective are fundamental tools in understanding how the dynamics of the options trading market works.

Chapter 1: What are Options?

In this chapter, we are going to drill down on the basics of options and how these types of investments work in the overall scheme of financial markets. It must be pointed out that options are not investment vehicles in themselves.

What does that mean?

For example, when you purchase a stock, you're purchasing a piece of a company. That is, you are purchasing partial ownership of a publicly traded company. And while stock is not a tangible asset which you can hold in your hands, it is proof that you own a hard asset, in this case, a company.

So, when dealing with options, you are dealing with a number of transactions which have an underlying asset supporting them. However, this type of investment fits the description and definition of a derivative. This is why the options trading market tends to be a bit more complex than the traditional equities market.

But before we dig any deeper into options themselves, let's get some important definitions out of the way.

First of all, this book does not deal in securities trading. As such, we are not talking about stocks and bonds. When you talk about securities in general, you are talking about ownership of real assets which you can then convert into cash in the regular markets.

For instance, if you purchase stock in a company, you can then turn around and sell that stock to another investor. Whether you make or lose money is dependent on market forces. Consequently, you must be clear on what price you are purchasing a security and at what price you are going to be selling it. Nevertheless, stocks are highly liquid assets because you can trade them virtually anytime you want, and you will always find a buyer for them.

Unless you have purchased stock into a company that has completely tanked, you will always find investors who are willing to take on stock even in a down market. This is what I mean when I say that stocks are highly liquid assets.

Another type of highly liquid assets contained under the securities umbrella is bonds. Bonds are also highly liquid assets that can be sold immediately when you need cash. Of course, if you have purchased bonds of a nation which is in default, then such bonds will essentially be worthless. So long as you invest in high-quality bonds, you will always have an asset which you can convert into cash at any moment.

With this definition, I hope to illustrate what a security is. Please feel free to check out any of the other books in this series which deal on the topic of equities markets and stock trading. I am sure these books will provide you with a wealth of information that you can put to use right away as you find your bearings as an investor.

One other thing before we move on to defining what an option is, trading in options is a speculative activity that yields good results but does not come without significant risk. That is why I would encourage you to do your homework at all times so that you are sure that the investments you are making will provide you with the opportunity to protect yourself against such risks.

Defining "Options"

An option, simply put, is a financial contract that locks in the right to buy or sell but not an obligation.

What this implies, is that an option is exactly as what its name suggests: it is a choice, not an obligation. As such, you as an investor can choose to lock in a given price for the contract, but you are not obligated to carry out with the transaction.

As a result, you have the option of backing out of the contract if, for some reason, you choose to do so. For instance, it could be that you have a cash flow problem and you run out of money. So, you can't go through with the contract unless you find the money to make the deal happen.

Granted, most transactions in the derivatives market don't necessarily involve cash, but you do need to have some type of liquidity in order to make the deal go through. In other cases, circumstances change, and you may no longer become interested in that particular asset which you took the option out on.

Now, the reason why we say that options are derivatives is because you are not actually trading the asset itself, but rather, you are entering a contract which is based on an underlying asset. Since an option is a contract in which you have the right to buy or sell—that is one contract, the actual purchase or sale is a separate contract.

I hope you can see that when an option goes through, it is actually two, separate contracts that kick in. The reason for this is because you could actually make the deal without enacting the options contract.

Allow me to illustrate.

Let's assume that your company does a lot of business overseas. It is based in the US and the majority of its business is in Europe. So, your company is naturally worried about exchanged rates between the US Dollar and the Euro. Since there is a high degree of uncertainty surrounding the Euro at the moment due to the Brexit, you are concern about exchange rates affecting your business deals.

In two months, you will collect a sizeable sum of money which will come due as per the expiration of a contract. Your business partner will make the payment in Euros as per the agreement. But your company is concerned that if the Euro falls because of the Brexit, then you will actually be left with less money once you convert it back to US Dollars.

In other words, if the Euro tanks, you will receive less US dollars when you convert that payment from Euros back into US Dollars.

Therefore, this concern has led your company's directors to consider taking out an options contract with a local financial institution that will underwrite the contract locking in a fixed exchange rate. What this does is protect your company's income in case the Euro should tank.

Consequently, there are two possible outcomes: one, the Euro tanks, and the other, the Euro doesn't tank.

Let's assume the first: the Euro tanks.

On the day you took out the contract, the USD–EUR exchange rate was 1.30 – 1. That is, $1.30 for €1. Thus, if the company receives €1,000 this would equal $769.23. If the Euro tanks and the exchange rate levels off, then you might reach parity between the US Dollar and the Euro at a 1-for-1 exchange. In this case, the US-based company wins as they receive more Dollars for each Euro it receives. This would be a positive outcome for the company.

Let's take a look at the second scenario: the Euro doesn't tank, in fact, it gains in value.

Since we are discussing the possibility of Brexit, it could be that the Pound Sterling tanks and UK investor drop the Pound like hot coal and jump into the Euro. Under this scenario, the value of the Euro would skyrocket. This is the scenario your company was worried about.

So, your company took out the options contract hoping that it would be covered should the worst happen. For the sake of illustration, let's assume that the USD-EUR exchange rate goes to $2 for €1. In this case, €1,000 suddenly becomes $500.

As you can see, this scenario is about a bad as it could get. It would not only represent a serious loss in terms of USD, but there is no guarantee that it could actually be the exchange; after all, it could jump to $2.50 for €1. With exchange rates, you never know how it could play out.

So, your company gets its local bank to underwrite the contract setting the exchange at $1.45 for €1 since you figure you can deal with the drop of 15 points on the Dollar, but not more. The bank is happy to underwrite at that rate because they figure they wouldn't lose money on the deal. In the worst of cases, they dump a bunch of Dollars and keep the more valuable Euros.

In the event that the Euro tanks, you won't need the contract. Your bank will thank you for your business and charge you a flat processing fee simply for underwriting the contract. Basically, it's just to cover whatever was paid to the underwriters for drafting up the contract.

But, let's assume that the Euro doesn't tank and it shoots up to the moon. Let's consider the Euro going to $2.50 for €1. In that case, you thank your lucky stars that you had that option. It kicks into gear, the bank pays out the exchange rate at $1.45 for €1 and you don't take a serious hit. In addition, the bank will charge you 1% on the total of the transaction to cover its administrative expenses.

In this example, you engaged in a derivatives contract since the contract itself was only to agree on a price for the currency to be exchanged. You didn't sign a contract for the currency itself. That is a separate transaction that is governed by a different contract.

At the end of the day, you are betting on something happening, or not. That is what derivatives are all about. Banks act like bookies in which they take in a bunch of bets, let things play out, and then collect when the bets are done.

It should also be said that this type of transaction is highly risky for all those involved as there could be any number of factors involved in the deal. So, if something should go wrong, it will go wrong for a lot of people... and really fast.

Options Basics

So now that we have a better understanding of what options are and how it essentially works, it should be noted that this currency transaction is only one example of the type of options contracts which you can become involved in.

Consequently, you need to be aware of the different types of transactions that may happen at any given time. It is up to the managers of a company to understand the risks the company is exposed to and how options can be used to hedge their position.

Often, you will hear the word "hedge" being used to refer to protecting your position against potential risks that may arise from uncertain conditions in the economy, political situations, or even disruptions in the supply of commodities such as oil and gas.

On the surface, there are different types of options such as Exchange Traded Funds (ETFs), which are very popular with commodities such as oil and gas, futures contracts, again very popular with commodities, equities, bonds, and currency, among others.

These types of contracts, as I have mentioned, do not represent the actual underlying asset in any way. You are not actually purchasing an asset unless you engage in a contract such as futures contracts in which you are locking in today's price for tomorrow's production of a specific commodity.

Although you need to be aware as not all futures contracts will specific physical delivery of the commodity. For instance, oil futures lock in a price today for the oil production that will be delivered three months from now. But I am not an oil refinery. So, I don't have any need for the actual physical oil. So, what I can do is let the contract mature. When I am ready to take physical delivery, I can turn around and sell the same oil at a different price, hopefully higher, to a company which actually needs to the oil to produce their products.

This example underscores how you need to be aware if the contract actually stipulates physical delivery. As with most ETFs, you will not get physical delivery of the underlying asset. What you will get is a check for the price of that asset. It is debatable whether the asset itself is more valuable than the cash. However, there are many scenarios in which cash would be worthless and the commodities would be king.

While that's a topic for another day, it's worth noting that options can help you hedge against the worst case scenario situations you have identified as part of your forecasting. As an investor, it could be a chance to capitalize on potential market fluctuations.

The Mechanics of Options

In essence, options are underwritten by financial institutions that are duly registered and supervised by the Securities and Exchange Commission (SEC) and are subject to a series of financial and banking regulations. The SEC is in charge of making sure that no monkey business is going and that all financial institutions comply with the regulations set forth in applicable legislations.

That being said, options are contracts between two parties (though it is possible for multiple parties to become involved) which agree on the price, term, assets, and other conditions that will trigger the contract.

Since the essence of an option is that it is optional, and thereby not forcing the parties to follow through, there are ground rules that govern the actual process of the contract.

For instance, there may be *force majeure* clauses which would void the contract in case of a serious and unexpected event such as a terrorist attack, natural disaster, or some other unforeseen event. These clauses can be included as provisions to protect the parties involved.

Beyond that, there are standard clauses that stipulate that the parties may withdraw from the contract prior 48-hour notice, or the parties might have to pay a certain amount of money for withdrawing from the contract altogether.

The fact of the matter is that each contract is different and contemplates different circumstances as provided for in the text itself. Once the contract is approved and signed, it is notarized and registered with the SEC. This gives the contract public faith.

If, and when, the contract is enacted, the parties must follow through on what is agreed, and everyone goes home happy. If the contract is not enacted, then the deal is off the table and everyone walks away.

Call Options

The first of the two general types of options we are going to be talking about are the "call options".

In short, a call gives the holder of the contract the right to buy the underlying asset but does not have the obligation to do so.

Now, let's break down this definition further.

First of all, call options are put into place when an investor is looking to purchase at a specified price. In that case, you could be tracking the price of any security, derivative, or basically any type of financial instrument.

So, when an investor decides to put this option in, the stock broker will become aware of this intention and inform the investor that the asset has fallen to the desired price. When this happens, the call option can be enacted, and the purchase goes through.

In the days of manual trading in which most orders were phoned in, investors and brokers usually had standing agreements. They would execute the options by phone and then sign the paperwork after the fact just so they could have legal backing.

With the advent of electronic trading, brokers and investors don't need to phone in their options. They can pre-program their electronic trading software and make the deal. This makes trading a lot faster and it allows for a greater number of transactions to be carried out in a single day.

But there's a catch—when traders put in their call options, they will set them at a specific price. So, when that security falls to that price, the buy order is immediately generated, and the security is sold. No questions asked. This is done because the option had already been set up that way.

Of course, the trader could kill the option if they feel the price will rebound. But it's important to note that if you are going to be exercising options, then you need to be at the wheel the whole time. If you do fall asleep at the wheel, then you might find yourself in a tough spot.

Put Options

Put options are the opposite of call options. These options give the holder the right to sell but not the obligation to do so.

Again, both investors and brokers will have standing agreements as part of the business they do. If an investor hires a professional portfolio manager, then the manager will have *carte blanche* to do as they see fit. This means that the need to call in orders is not needed.

Just like call options, put options can be programmed through electronic trading platforms, either run by individual investors or portfolio managers. The sell order is triggered when the underlying asset reaches a specific price. Of course, orders can be canceled, but the broker needs to be ready to do so.

Let's look at a practical example that will illustrate how both types of options work.

Let's assume that the underlying asset is a stock. The asset is "X" number of shares for ABC Company. The current share price for ABC Company is $10 per share. Since this is a solid company, investors are interested in purchasing more stock. However, the current sale price is a bit too high for their liking. So, a call option is placed for this stock. The buy order will be triggered when the asset reaches $9 per share.

So, let's assume that it does. The buy order is triggered for 100 shares at $9 apiece. Voila! The trade has been made.

Conversely, those who are holding the shares of ABC Company have decided they are willing to share if the price jumps to $11 per share. When this happens, the sell order is automatically triggered, and the stock is sold.

As such, let's say that it does happen. The share price of ABC jumps to $11. Consequently, the sell order is executed, and the sale goes through.

In this example, the investors who want to buy are waiting for the price of the stock to fall to a point where they feel comfortable. In contrast, the holders of the stock are willing to sell, if and when, the stock reaches a level they too feel comfortable with.

This example works with round figures for the sake of simplicity. In the real world, share prices often have a trading range of a few cents per share. However, when you multiply a few cents over a few thousand shares, then you are making sizeable income on every trade.

Options contracts

As I mentioned earlier, options are contracts. Despite the fact that they are legally binding, thus meaning you could get sued over breach of contract, you are not obligated to go through with the sale or purchase of the underlying asset.

The reason for this is that investors wanted to give themselves some leeway in case circumstance changed unexpectedly. And believe me, they do change in a hurry. So the best thing to keep in mind is that an option is there to protect you from any possible negative outcomes. However, you must be ready to act in case something goes wrong.

Valuation of Options

This is the tricky part.

Valuation of the derivatives market is largely a guessing game. Most statistical models used to value derivatives are mainly statistical models that factor in trading averages and other input factors such time, supply of the asset, inflation, exchange rates, and well, you can imagine that some of these models get pretty complex.

However, the basic element which determines the valuation of assets and options is supply and demand. When a security or commodity is under intense pressure from a lack of supply, prices will skyrocket as investors seek to lock in their prices before they reach the moon.

This usually triggers a healthy number of options, both call and put, since everyone is looking to get a good deal. Those that hold the security or commodity would like to sell when the price is at its highest point, while buyers will be looking to get in before the price of the security or commodity reaches its peak.

At this point, electronic trading can wreak havoc on the price of an asset since the market can be flooded in a matter of minutes with sell orders and kill the price of the asset, or become inundated with buy order and push the price up through the roof.

For most investors, valuing options is about making bets and having the cash and credit to cover them in case they lose. So, it pays to do your homework and make sure that whatever happens, you are ready to make the call, or kill the deal before it happens.

Please bear in mind that the valuation of derivatives is based largely on suppositions about what could, or could not happen. As such, it's important to consider the circumstances which you might be facing ahead of making a decision.

Since there is really no way to predict how high, or how low, the price of an asset will go, then you must be aware to make deals happen at the right time. I encourage folks to sell when they feel they are comfortable with the profit they are going to make, and buy at a point where they feel they are going to make money on the upswing.

Your best bet is to become familiar with market averages. There is the two-day market average, 10-day, 50-day, and 200-day averages. Of course, there are others such as one-year, two-year, five-year, or even longer averages. But those types of averages serve better as historical data rather than data that will be used to base trading decisions.

Therefore, you must become familiar with these averages so that you can get a sense of where prices are tending (either upward or downward). Don't be fooled by sudden spikes or drops. These fluctuations are a normal part of trading. Unless you are a day trader, short-term effects should have no bearing on the overall trend you are seeing in the data.

Now, if you are involved in highly-speculative short-term trading, then the two-day average is the one you want to look at. But if you are in it for the long haul, then longer data sets will help you improve your decision-making abilities.

Summary

In this chapter, we went over options. We stated that options are contracts which give the holder the right to buy or sell, but not the obligation to do so.

The valuation of options, despite the use of complex statistical modeling, is largely based on supply and demand. As such, if you are familiar with the trends in the price of the securities or commodities you are looking to trade, then you can be sure that you are going to make considerable gains.

Otherwise, you had better consider the option of hiring a professional portfolio manager who can make the best investment decisions for you. At the end of the day, doing your homework is essential in determining what the best course of action may be for you and for your portfolio.

I would highly advise you to seek professional advice before putting your money into place. Consequently, you will put yourself in a position to be successful while managing your risk as best as you possibly can.

Finally, it pays to become familiar with technical analysis, that is, the use of quantitative data that can allow you to make informed decisions based on the data sets available, especially if there are healthy sets of historical data available.

So, please bear in mind that research is one of the core elements to any successful trader. Be aware of falling asleep at the wheel as this may cause you to

lose control of the ship and hit an iceberg that's
hidden somewhere underneath the water.

Chapter 2: Different Types of Options

In the previous chapter, we went over the general guidelines as to what options are. We drilled down into how options can be used. In addition, we discussed a sample exercise that will allow you to better understand how options work in the financial world.

In this chapter, we will focus on the different types of options contracts and how these may vary according to the different provisions that are included in their drafting. This implies that there is a myriad of options in addition to the standard call and put options.

Various Options Markets

It is important to note that options are not exclusive to one market or one country. Options are a worldwide phenomenon, though the laws and regulations to these contracts do vary from country to country.

As such, investors based in the United States will have to comply with the rules and regulations set forth by the SEC. This is a different situation in Europe as each country sets forth a different set of regulations governing the issuance of options trades.

In a nutshell, it boils down to the individual brokerage firms that handle this type of transactions. So, large multinational banks are governed by the laws of the country in which they are based, and if conducting operations overseas, they are also governed by applicable international banking regulations such as BASILEA, and the local laws of the other party's home country.

As you can see, this is a complex endeavor since there are applicable laws from all parts of the world and not just one, host country. At the end of the day, it pays for both investors and brokers to do their due diligence in order to avoid potential legal complications.

One other consideration on the various options markets, many of the transactions conducted in the derivatives market are usually insured by a secondary insurance company that provides coverage to large deals. Often, these insurance companies also have a multinational presence. Therefore, these insurance firms must also comply with applicable legislation.

In order to simplify contracts, the contract may stipulate that the contract itself is governed by the laws of a specific nation. In which case, any disputes and issues must be resolved in the jurisdiction indicated in the contract itself. However, the laws of each individual nation still apply especially in case there is any criminal wrongdoing which may lead to indictments. Of course, this is a bit of an extreme case, but it serves to highlight the legal ramifications of these types of deals.

Different Types of Options Contracts

So, let's take a look at the different types of options contracts out there in the market today.

Call options

As discussed earlier, these are contracts which trigger a purchase order at a specified price.

Put options

Also, these contracts triggers sell orders when an asset reaches a specified price. There are two interesting variations on this type of contract.

The so-called "stop-loss" order is used when the price of an asset falls below the break-even point for a particular deal. In this case, the investor decides how much they are willing to lose before making a deal to sell. In this case, the reason for holding on to a stock despite it losing money is due to the hope of it bouncing back.

The other variation is the "minimum gain", that is, the least that you are willing to accept as a profit. So, you will not sell unless the asset reaches a certain price. Even if you are making money on the deal, the holder of the security is prepared to forego this profit unless the asset reaches the specified price in the option.

American style

No, we're not talking about hamburgers here.

An American style contract offers a good deal of flexibility, especially in terms of a contract's expiration date. American-style contracts allow for deals to be made ahead of the contract's expiration or right at the expiration. This offers much greater flexibility as investors don't necessarily have to wait for the asset's price to reach a certain point or wait until the contract is up.

European style

This is a much more restrictive contract. Typically, European-style contracts do not allow for trades to be made ahead of the contract's expiration or at different price points than the agreed one.

This type of contract offers more security in terms of having clear rules and provisions, though it does make transaction somewhat riskier if there are no *force majeure* clauses included.

Exchange traded options

These contracts are those which are listed in public stock exchanges such as the New York Stock Exchange or the Chicago Stock Exchange. As their name suggests, these options are public. So, anyone can buy into them, and cash out at any time. These options must be conducted through a duly registered and supervised broker.

Unlike private options trades, in which any parties can engage in them, publicly traded options must comply with the rule and regulations of the land.

The most famous of these types of contracts is the Exchange Traded Funds (ETFs) mentioned earlier. ETFs usually have an underlying asset, a commodity, which can be bought into by any investor who chooses to invest in that fund.

These funds are offered by duly registered and supervised financial entities and are managed by professional money managers. Since these managers are sworn to uphold their fiduciary obligation, they will do their best to protect their investor's money. Otherwise, they could be disbarred, face severe penalties, and even incarceration.

ETFs are good investment vehicles for those who want exposure to commodities with the means to diversify their portfolio but are not actually interested in physical delivery of the underlying asset. A good example of this is an oil ETF. Unless you want barrels of oil showing up at your doorsteps, you're better off just collecting a check for your winnings.

Options Classified by Underlying Asset

Thus far, we have talked about underlying assets in options contracts. So, let's take a look at the different types of underlying assets.

- **Stock options** – This option holds the underlying asset as stock in publicly traded companies.

- **Index options** – These are basically the same as a stock option, except that these options track a stock index such as the Dow Jones or Nasdaq. As such, the underlying asset is the stock of a group of companies rather than one, individual company.

- **FOREX** – These are options in the currency market. These could be like the first example we provided in the introduction of this book, or it could be directly in the currency exchange market. This is a highly speculative and risky market. It is definitely not for beginners nor the faint of heart.

- **Futures contracts** – This type of option enables investors to lock in the price of a commodity at present while taking delivery of such commodities at a later date. This is ideal when price fluctuations are taken into account. Futures also apply to currencies.

- **Commodity options** - The commodities involved in this type of contract can be any type of commodity so long as there is a mechanism which can set the price fairly.

- **Basket options** - In this case, the underlying asset is not just one, or one type of asset. Rather, it can be several assets including commodities, stocks, and bonds. These types of investment vehicles are created with the intent to hedge risk through diversification.

Options by Date of Expiration

In this type of contract, options are classified by their date of expiration and not by price or any other provisions contained in the contract. This means that the contract will only be enacted so long as the term is met.

It's worth noting that contracts do not follow a template that is set in stone, but rather, they follow general guidelines which provide their structure.

As such, options contracts by date have the following characteristics:

- **Regular options**. These contracts generally last 30 days unless otherwise stated. This tends to be the default term on options contracts, though provisions can be included to address specific terms or extensions given market conditions and so on.

- **Weekly options**. Just as its name indicates, weekly options have a 7-day term attached to them. These are ideal for investors who are trading in the short term. Also, these options are a staple of high-frequency trading in which many trades are conducted on a regular basis.

- **Quarterly options**. These contracts have an expiration date attached to a quarter, that is, a three-month period. These are more common with longer-term traders and investors. This type of option provides more flexibility when tracking the price of a security or a commodity during a longer period of time.

- **Long-term Expiration Anticipation Securities**. Also known as LEAPS, they are available for a wide array of securities over a much longer term. LEAPS can be bought at any time in the year but always expire in January. They can be bought for periods of up to three years.

- **Employee stock options.** These types of contracts are offered in lieu of increased monetary compensation or as an incentive for employees to become more committed in the company. These are called options because employees have the choice to hold or sell their stake in the company's equity. Since the financial scandals that rocked the financial industry in the early 2000s, employee stock options have been heavily regulated.

- **Cash settled options.** In this type of contract, the parties may choose to settle the transaction of the underlying asset with cash instead of the asset itself. This is common with ETFs. It's important to read the fine print with ETFs as there may be specific provisions that commodities included as underlying assets may be "unallocated" which means that the holder will never receive the actual, physical asset, but rather, its equivalent in cash.

- **Exotic options.** With these contracts, there are specific provisions that are made to them which may include complex stipulations.

Therefore, there are a wide variety of exotic contracts. These are also known as Non-Standardized options in which they contain specific provisions that adjust to specific markets.

- **Barrier options**. For these contracts, the holder is paid if the underlying asset reaches a specific price, or not. This is very similar to the traditional call and put option with the difference that the transaction will be triggered as soon as the underlying security or commodity reaches the agreed price or not, hence, the difference. With traditional calls and puts, the sell or buy order is placed when the actual price triggers it.

- **Binary options**. This contract contemplates a payout to the holder if, and when, the contract expires with a profit to the holder. The payout is generally in monetary terms.

- **Chooser options**. The name for this contract is derived from the fact that the holder may choose to convert the contract into a call or put at the expiration of the contract. In essence, the holder decides what is best for them at the expiration of the contract.

- **Compound options.** This is called "compound" since the underlying asset is another options contract.

- **Look Back Options.** In this case, there is no fixed price, but rather, the holder of the contract may choose the best price for the underlying asset as seen throughout the term of the contract. This is frequently used with currencies.

Benefits of Options

Options offer a series of benefits to their holders. But also, options provide mutual benefit to all parties involved so long as all sides are able to adequately manage risk and understand the valuation of the underlying assets. Here are some of the main benefits of options.

1. They offer flexibility to investors and financial firms.
2. Investors can hedge risk by locking in prices through futures contracts.
3. Companies and individuals can protect themselves against fluctuations in currency prices.

4. Contracts can be negotiated based on the specific needs of all parties.
5. Contracts can be settled in cash without actually having to settle in the underlying asset.

These are the main benefits that options can provide investors. It's important to note that the underlying assets which give support to these contracts should be thoroughly researched in order to understand where potential risk may lie.

Potential Risks of Options

Risk is an inherent part of any trading done in the derivatives market. As such, it is important for investors to understand such risks. Given this condition, here are some of the most relevant risks that may affect options contracts.

1. Market volatility as seen in violent swings in asset prices.
2. Lack of supply in order to guarantee delivery of a physical asset.
3. Cases of insolvency or illiquidity on the part of investors.
4. Incorrect valuation due to a lack of understanding of the underlying asset.
5. Inappropriate term of contract due to a lack of foresight.

These risks can be remedied by a thorough understanding of the underlying assets and how these can be used to leverage these contracts. Consequently, investors need to be aware of such risk. By understanding risks and potential pitfalls, investors can ensure that they are covered in case any unforeseen events should take place.

Chapter 3: Technical Options Terminology

In this chapter, we are going to be taking a closer look at some terms and definitions related to options trading. This terminology is intended to give a quick reference guide for whenever you have any questions about any specific terms or definitions.

Therefore, it is important for you to become familiar with these terms as they commonly come up within the investment world. Also, some of these expressions have a cross-cutting appeal, as they are not exclusive to options trading, but may be found in all sorts of trading situations.

So, we're going to drill down into each one of these in alphabetical order.

Asian Option

In this type of option, the payout in the contract is dependent upon the average price of the underlying asset over a given period of time (for example, a week, or a month) as opposed to the European and American options which depend on the maturity of the contract.

Asset Swap

In a derivatives contract, two parties may choose to simply swap assets regardless of price or any other underlying factor. This type of contract is very useful in cases in which both parties are in need of acquiring one asset and are perfectly willing to part with the other. For example, both parties may switch a specific amount of currency regardless of the exchange rates.

Antedate

In legal contracts, the date is one which occurs prior to the maturity of the contract, or occurrence of the stipulations in the contract. It is also known as a "backdate".

Bear Call Spread

A bear call spread, also referred to a call credit spread, is a strategy in which an options contract is intended when there is an expected decline in the price of the underlying asset. This can be done by purchasing the option at a given strike price. Then, the asset is sold at the expiration date but at a lower price. The maximum profit which can be made is the same as the original credit received when beginning the trade.

Binary Option

In this type of option, the outcome of the option is considered upon a "yes/no" proposition and hence its binary nature. As such, the investor makes money at the expiration of the contract, then the investor is "in the money". If the investor loses money, then they are "out of the money". This contract depends solely on its expiration date and represents one large bet which could play out in one of two ways.

Breakeven Point

The breakeven point is the point in which the sale price of an underlying asset reaches its original cost. In other words, the investor makes their money back but does not make any profit on the sale of the original security or option.

Bull Call Spread

This is essentially the opposite of the bear call spread. In this option, the investor will purchase call options at a given strike price. Then, the investor will sell the options at a higher price upon the expiration date. Profit is to be made from the difference between the lower purchase price and the higher sell price.

Cash or Nothing Put

This is a type of exotic option in which there is a fixed price, often equal to the strike price, which serves to trigger the payout of the contract if the underlying asset's price falls below the strike price. Otherwise, the payout is zero.

Cash Trigger

This is the price point in which an investor has decided to trigger the buy/sell option of the contract. In this condition, the option will go through and the trade is completed.

Cash-settled Options

These options are settled in monetary terms, in the currency which is agreed upon, and not with actual physical delivery of the underlying asset. This is a common feature of ETFs.

Charm (Delta Decay)

"Charm" is the term which refers to the rate at which the delta of an option varies over time. It refers to the second order derivative of an option's valuation. This is considered as once to time and once to price. It can also be considered as a derivative of theta, the indicator which measures time decay of that option's valuation.

Contingency Order

A contingency order may be executed when specific conditions are met in an investor's portfolio. For instance, these may be executed when the investor is lacking funds and needs to sell in order to free up cash. In other cases, very specific conditions may be met in terms of depth and scope, which will trigger the option.

Contract Market

This is a board of trade, or an exchange, that has been designated to the trade of any given options or futures. These must be duly registered with its corresponding supervisory authority in the country in which it operates.

Date Certain

This term is used to refer to the exact date on which stipulated actions on a contract are to take place. As such, when the specified date is reached, the action is then executed as per the terms of the contract.

Deal Ticket

This is a record of all the term, conditions, and other pertinent information in an agreement. The deal ticket is generated after the transaction of the contracts takes place.

Delta-Gamma Hedging

This is a strategy in which both delta and gamma hedges are used in order to mitigate the risk involved with regard to the changes in an underlying asset and in the delta itself.

Early Exercise

This term refers to the execution of a buy or sell order in a contract prior to the expiration date. In this case, the contract may stipulate that the order be executed when the stipulated strike price is hit and not upon the maturity of the contract.

Exchange Traded Option

This is when individual investors may buy into a contract which is open on a publicly traded market under the strike price. The contract may be executed when either the contract matures or the strike price is hit.

Far Option

This type of option is the one with a longer expiration date contained in a calendar option spread. This option involves buying and selling options with different expiration dates. Under this model, the short spread is the nearest one in expiration while the long one has the farthest expiration date.

Extrinsic Value

This term refers to the difference in the market price of an option, also referred to as "premium" and its intrinsic value. Extrinsic value also refers to the part of an option's price which is not determined by factors pertaining to the contract's underlying asset, but rather, it is due to external factors.

Failure to Deliver

As its name suggests, this refers to when one of the parties involved in the contract does not meet their obligations. Penalties and other sanctions may be imposed as per the stipulations of the contract. In general, this is due when one party may not have the money to cover their position or the other is unable to deliver on the underlying asset.

Fiduciary Call

In a fiduciary call, parties use the option in order to execute a cost-effective strategy to limit the costs associated with the exercise of a call option. Consequently, when an investor exercises a call option, the investor must have the necessary funds to make the call when the time comes to make the purchase.

Floating Price

A floating price refers to a price which is not fixed, but rather, may fluctuate according to market conditions. This type of price is intended to address variations in market prices such as in commodities like oil and gas. This may also apply to exchange rates in the case of currency transactions.

Gamma

A gamma refers to the rate of change in an option's delta valuation. It refers to a one-point move in the underlying asset's price. Therefore, a dealt hedge is used to reduce the gamma in an option, so the option's price is maintained over time.

Illiquid Option

This is a contract which cannot be easily sold or transferred into cash in a short period of time in terms of the current market. This could be due to a number of factors. In essence, an option may be illiquid if the yield on the options are too low, or if there are stipulations in the contract which make it difficult to keep.

Lambda

This term refers to the ratio of change in the monetary price, usually in Dollars, of an option. It refers to the 1% change in the expected price volatility or implied volatility of the underlying asset. The lambda can be used to tell investors how much the price of an option will change given the changes in the implied volatility of the option's price.

Married Put

A married put is essentially an insurance policy for investors. This is a strategy in which an investor, who holds a long position, purchases an option known as "at the money" on the same asset, in order to protect themselves against the depreciation of the same asset's price.

Max Pain

This is the strike price of an underlying asset in an option that would cause financial loss to the investor in either a call or put option. Upon reaching their max pain point, investors may choose to get out of a contract and cut their losses.

Natural Hedge

This is a protection strategy which is used by investors and companies in order to protect themselves from currency fluctuations. For instance, they may choose to move operations to another country, or do business in a different currency, in order to avoid potential losses due to exchange rate volatility.

Non-Equity Option

These contracts refer to those which have assets other than securities as underlying assets. These assets could be currencies or commodities.

Omega

This Greek refers to the measurement of various characteristics of options. In particular, it measures the change of the underlying asset's price as compared to the price of the option itself.

One-touch Option

This type of contract pays a premium on the contract itself if the underlying's asset's market price reaches a specified point.

Outright Option

This refers to options which are bought and sold individually. In essence, this refers to any type of option bought and sold privately. This could be done between a bank and an investor. It is the basic type of option on an underlying asset. It can be either a call or put.

Over the Counter Market

Over the counter markets or OTC markets are those which do not have a specific physical location such as a given stock exchange. OTC markets can be traded by phone or email in which financial institutions trade with investors.

Perpetual Option

This is an exotic option which stipulates no maturity or time limit. The actual lifespan of a perpetual option may range from a few days to years. Its expiration is triggered by specific conditions such as the market price of the underlying asset. These options are agreed upon the parties based on their needs or expectations.

Physical Options

In this type of options contract, the underlying asset is a physical one in which the investors choose to take physical allocation of such underlying asset. With these contracts, investors may turn around and sell the physical asset or roll the option over.

Ratio Spread

This type of spread measures the ratio between long and short positions, that is, the number ratio of short positions as compared to the long ones. Typically, short positions will outnumber long ones 2 to 1.

Rolling Options

These contracts offer the investor the option to take the payout of the contract upon maturity or have extended the expiration of the contract thereby rolling it over. This allows investors to have flexibility both in term and market price. These options are preferred by investors who are feeling bullish on the price of the underlying asset.

Russian Option

Russian options generally do not have an expiration date and give the holder the option to sell at the best price during the lifespan of the contract. These are considered perpetual options and due to their nature, are also considered exotic options.

Spot Price

This term refers to the current price of an asset. It is the average of buy and sell prices over a given period of time. Spot price may also serve to determine the trigger in a contract.

Strike Price

The strike price is the price in which a contract can be exercised. The strike price can be different from the spot price of a security or commodity. In any event, the contract may stipulate the strike price when a specified spot price is reached.

Theta

This is another of the Greeks. In essence, theta measures the decline in the value of an option over a given period of time. Even if all factors remain constant, a contract still loses value over time as the contract draws closer to its maturity.

Time Decay

This term refers to the change in an option over a given period of time, generally, the maturity of the contract itself. Over time, options lose value for the sake of being open. This implies that the longer an option is open, the longer it loses value.

Uncovered Option

This term refers to options in which the investor buys into an option without holding a counter position. The investor may not hold a long position in the underlying asset or have the cash to cover the position. This is called a naked position. It is highly risky and may lead to insolvency on the part of the investor.

Underlying Asset

This is the asset, a security, bond, commodity, or any other asset, which serves as the support for the contract itself. This may be a physical asset or an intangible asset. Options may stipulate delivery of the underlying asset or may be settled in cash.

Vega

This is the measurement of the price sensitivity of the underlying asset of an options contract. Vega measures a 1% in the implied volatility of the underlying asset.

Wasting Asset

This refers to a depreciating asset that loses value over time even if it is not used. This is a type of fixed asset such as vehicles or machinery.

Zomma

Another of the Greek options. Zomma measures the change in gamma in relation to the changes in the volatility of an underlying asset.

These terms are some of the various terms you will come across throughout your journey into options trading. In particular, we have introduced the Greek terms which are associated with options trading. We will discuss these terms, their calculations in depth in a later chapter.

For now, I would encourage you to become familiar with these terms. Your understanding of these terms will help you become more proficient in your mastery of the options trading domain. So, it would certainly pay for you to do your homework as a part of your daily trading routine.

Chapter 4: Options Trading vs. Stock Trading

In this chapter, we are going to take a closer look at how securities trading differs from trading options. In particular, stocks, which are the most popular form of securities, are traded openly through various markets and means.

As such, most investors are familiar with stock trading but may not be too familiar at how options can be used, both in the equities market and on its own as a part of a broader investment strategy. Thus, it's imperative that investors become familiar with the various alternatives which are available to them as part of an overall investment strategy.

One other point that I would like to make is that diversification is a fundamental strategy which looks to hedge risk by spreading investable assets over various investment classes. Naturally, options are one type of investment class which investors can take advantage of.

It's also important to note that securities and options, while usually related to each other, are traded in different markets.

Since securities refer to stock of publicly traded companies, they are traded in primary markets in which they are presented to the investment public through financial firms which broker the trades of these stocks.

Consequently, investors work in tandem with these investment firms in order to buy and sell securities, either as individual purchases of stocks or through other investment vehicles such as mutual funds. Thus, investors have various ways in which they can gain exposure to the stock market.

Options are involved in the securities market, though they are not securities in themselves. As we have started earlier, options are considered derivatives since they don't trade assets as such. Instead, the options use assets as support for the contract itself.

This is why the term "underlying" asset is so commonly used when referring to options. Of course, a futures contract may ultimately lead to the purchase or sale of an asset. However, the option itself does not deal with the asset in question.

Since there is a myriad of options available, investors must be well aware of the choices they have available to them. The more investors become familiar with options, the better they will come to understand the opportunities that are available to them.

It should be noted that options trading is not for beginners and does require a certain level of proficiency. While you may not need to hold a Ph.D. in finance and economics to trade in options, it is worthwhile to take the time to study in order to truly comprehend what is behind this type of financial instrument.

In addition, I would encourage you to seek professional financial advice while you become proficient in your trading skills. That way, you can compare your understanding of financial instruments and investments with that of licensed professionals. In fact, the worst thing that could happen is you pay a professional for a few hours of their time, but you end up learning about financial markets from experts who have experience in the game.

Overview of Equities Trading

So, let's take a look at how equities trading actually work.

In this discussion, we are going to focus solely on equities. We are not going to be discussing bonds or commodities as we are being explicit about comparing equities and options. This is an important distinction I would like to make since bonds and commodities, while falling under the securities umbrella, are completely different types of investments and have their own nuances. As such, discussing them implies an entirely different subject.

Thus, equities are the stock of publicly traded companies. A company "goes public" when it files to be listed on one of the stock exchanges located in their home country of operation. This is important to note since there are stock exchanges all over the world.

For instance, virtually every developed nation in the world has its own stock market in which publicly traded companies are listed. This is a fundamental requirement as company stock may not be traded without going through an exchange unless there is a specific contract offering individual investors direct sales of stock.

Now, for the sake of simplicity, we are going to use the United States as an example. However, if you are interested in trading in other countries, I would highly encourage you to read up on that particular market's laws and regulations as they may vary from country to country.

That being said, there are several stock exchanges throughout the United States. The most popular stock exchange is the New York Stock Exchange. This is the physical building in which stocks are traded. You may have seen the famous trading floor scenes in Hollywood films and television shows.

Now, there are two major players in all stock markets. There are the investors, and there are the investment firms which broker the sale of stock to the investing public. This is needed due to the regulations in US law which stipulates that licensed brokers are the ones who must facilitate the purchase and sale of publicly traded stock.

The reason for this is that there are several regulations which supervise the actions carried out by players in financial markets. As such, the law restricts the ways in which publicly traded companies may sell their stock to private investors.

It's worth mentioning that this applies to publicly traded companies since private companies, those which are not traded on any stock exchange, are free to do as they see fit with their company's stock.

When a private company chooses to go public, it must do so through a duly registered investment firm. Typically, these investment firms are large banks which deal with these types of transactions. The investment firm then underwrites the Initial Public Offering (IPO) of this company.

In an IPO, a private company, which will go public for the first time ever, will place their shares on sale to the investing public. The investment firm will then set a share price based on what they believe will be the best price investors will pay.

Now, depending on the company going public, investors may line up to get their hands on the IPO. Of course, the firm that's underwriting the IPO will have its own customers who will most likely get first dibs on the IPO.

Once the paperwork is completed and the IPO gets the green light, the newly traded company will hit the trading floor. At this point, the first wave of investors that gets their hands on the IPO must pony up the cash for the sale of the stock.

Then, the first wave of investors may choose to sell at any time they see fit. If the company is a hot-ticket item, they may choose to hold on a bit while the price goes up. When this happens, the investors that got into the IPO will clean up. The reason for this is that the investors who get into the IPO will pay a much lower price than what the market may be willing to pay.

After a company's IPO, they will be traded as part of the usual operations on a stock exchange. And consequently, are subject to options contracts as investors begin to consider this newly-listed corporation as an investment choice.

Valuation of Stocks

One of the most common questions in stock trading is the valuation of stocks.

The valuation of stocks is a highly psychological and emotional situation as investors may lose their cool and overpay for a stock that's "hot" while there may be companies whose stock is absolutely worthless.

In essence, stock prices are quoted as individual share prices, that is, the price of a single share of a publicly traded company. Your average, run-of-the-mill publicly traded corporation may have millions of outstanding shares which make up its share capital. In this case, the price of an individual share may be multiplied by the millions of outstanding shares thus arriving at its total share capital.

The individual share price is essentially determined by supply and demand. When a stock is hot, but there is a limited supply of shares available, then the price will go up as investors are willing to pay more and more for each share.

On the contrary, if there is little demand for a given stock, prices will fall as sellers need to lower their price to a point where they can entice other investors to buy. The reasons for a stock price to fall may vary, but in general, they are a sign that something is not sitting well with investors.

Therefore, the price that you see quoted on the nightly news is the result of the average between the buy and sell prices that investors are paying. As such, you may not necessarily get the price that you see quoted. It could be that you might get a lower price, but you must also note that you might get a higher price, as well.

The Role of the Stockbroker

The stockbroker is the individual who conducts the transactions on the equities market. This is the person whose name appears on the file for each individual trade. Brokers will charge a commission on each trade that they make.

This commission may range from a few cents on the Dollar (this is true of high-frequency trading) to a few Dollars per trade. So, commissions can add up when you conduct a large number of trades.

Also, brokers make money when deals make money. This is the case of mutual funds. For instance, a mutual fund is an amount of money pooled from different investors. All of the investors in the pool receive a return on their money. So, let's assume the return is 3% annually. The investor will make 3% on their money. It is now the job of the broker, or portfolio manager, to make over 3% in order to make more money for themselves.

This last point illustrates how brokers can become aggressive when looking to make more money for their investments. In addition, individual brokers and firms will look to pay as little as they can in order to maximize their own profits.

Investing in Stocks

It should be said that stock trading is not for everyone.

Most folks who would like to get exposure into the stock market may choose to purchase mutual funds from their local bank, or perhaps buy into their own company's stock option plan. In such cases, funds are managed by professional money managers who have experience and knowledge in the field. With these money or portfolio, managers might make mistakes from time to time, they generally make money most of the time.

This approach is generally what most folks go for as they may not have the time nor the expertise to engage in stock trading themselves. Nevertheless, it's important for you to become familiar with the way the stock market works as you will have an understanding of how your stock portfolio is performing given the conditions of the market.

Furthermore, a solid understanding of the investment options available to you will help you determine if the advice you are getting from a portfolio manager is really the best option that is available to you, or if there are other options that have not been considered. So, as always, it pays to do your homework.

Long Term versus Short Term

One of the other considerations that investors must keep in mind is if they are looking to engage in short-term trading or long-term trading.

A general rule of thumb is that the younger the investor, the longer they have to ride out the fluctuations in the markets. So, if an investor starts out in their 20s, they will have about 24 to 40 years of investing time before they plan to retire. So, if the markets have a couple of down years here and there, it won't derail their investments barring an unprecedented collapse.

On the other hand, older investors, say in their 40s or even 50s, may choose to engage in riskier trading strategies as they need to make up for lost time. In this scenario, a long-term approach means that you won't be engaging in quite as many trades as you would if you were looking to invest in the short term. Therefore, short-term investors generally make more trades than long-term investors do.

My advice to folks who are starting out in the investment world is to think about why you are looking to invest in the first place. So, if you are simply looking to get rich, then you might consider a short-term strategy, such as day trading in order to find the best way of making a good chunk of money.

Conversely, if you are thinking about investing for retirement, then you might look into a long-term approach in which you are more risk-averse and looking to keep your money invested longer so that you can maximize your returns over the long-term.

You will get rich with either strategy. The big difference is the time in between and the risk involved. While long-term investing espouses a slowly but surely approach, short-term trading espouses a much more aggressive approach which may open you up to more risk. As such, risk might imply that you could lose your shirt in a bad deal.

So, I would advise you to sit down and go over your goals. Whatever they are, this book will surely help you arrive at a good conclusion as to how you can use options trading to help you achieve your financial goals.

Benefits of Trading Equities

When you are looking to gain exposure into the equities market, it essentially boils down to risk. Since there is a myriad of options in which you can start off with a small amount of money, you don't need to be a wealthy millionaire to get into the stock market. But you do have to be aware of how risk can play out in the equities market.

As such, trading in equities is one of the safest ways in which you can invest your money. Sure, there is always risk involved in any type of deal. And as long as you don't have a maverick portfolio manager, your money should be safe.

For investors who are looking to gain exposure to the stock market but may be more risk-averse, there are several options available.

First, there are mutual funds. As I have stated before, a mutual fund is essentially a pool of money collected from different investors. This pool of money is then taken by the investment firm that sells it and assigned to a professional portfolio or money manager. This manager will then allocate the money into the various investment vehicles that are available.

When you look into purchasing a mutual fund, there are various types.

For example, you might buy into a mutual fund that is solely invested in stocks. This fund may be focused on a general basket of stocks such as blue-chip companies like IBM, Apple, Microsoft, and so on, or perhaps on industrial companies in the areas of steel and automobiles.

Also, mutual funds may be traded as index funds. These funds track specific stock indices such as the Dow Jones or the Nasdaq. In short, a stock index is a basket of companies which are grouped together and tracked as a whole. That means that the companies in that stock index represent a group thus providing a point of reference in the performance of these companies.

The Dow Jones, for example, groups the 30 largest companies in the United States. So, an index fund that is attached to the Dow would depend on the overall performance of the Dow. This means that if the Dow is up, the fund makes money. If the Dow is down, then the fund may lose money. As such, index funds may provide a great opportunity to make money in stocks without engaging in any risky practices.

Another advantage of trading equities is that there is a myriad of investment vehicles which you can select in order to get started. That means that you don't need to have millions of dollars to get started. There are mutual funds and other investment accounts in which you can get started with as little as $100 and then make monthly contributions to the account. This is a great way for you to gain exposure into stocks without actually having to invest a large lump sum of cash.

In addition, there are other safer investments vehicles such as certificates of deposit in which investor essentially deposit money into a bank account. Then, the bank issues a certificate to which the investor has the right to collect at its maturity.

In this type of investment vehicle, the investor doesn't need to do much except check up on their monthly statement. This allows investors to have a safer investment option though the returns may not be as high as other riskier options.

Finally, it's important to note that equities allow for a high degree of flexibility and diversification. So, if you are looking to gain exposure to a wide range of companies, industries, and sectors, equities can provide you with solid investment opportunities. A good diversification strategy can help you hedge risk while considering decent returns based on market expectations.

Drawbacks of Trading Equities

By far, the biggest drawback of trading in equities is the risk of volatility.

Volatility means that there is a risk of wild fluctuations in the prices of individual stocks or major stock indices. While having a diversified strategy would limit your overall risk, there is always the possibility that one company you have invested in takes a beating, or the overall economy begins to slow down.

That is why the term "recession" is a boogeyman term that scares the living daylights out of most investors. Recessions imply a bear market, which in turn, means that the overall markets will be down from their previous highs. Thus, investors need to be aware of the fact that they may end up taking a hit in their investments or even losing money. While the prospect of losing money is never fun, those investors who are in for the long haul may take market downturns in stride as opposed to those who are more focused on a short-term strategy.

Furthermore, novice investors will find it hard to uncover the best investment opportunities that are available to them. Naturally, finding the right opportunities is a question of time and patience. As a result, many investors simply don't have the time and the freedom to do the research that is needed in order to find solid companies out there.

You could cut corners a bit by purchasing a premium data and information package from a large investment firm. These information packages contain stats, analytics, insider information, and any other data which may help investors make informed decisions. On the whole, relying on the information published by these business intelligence units is useful, though it should not be the only sources to guide your decisions.

Hence, a lack of information is one of the biggest drawbacks in the equities market. There isn't always an abundance of information. Consequently, many investors lack the overall insight needed in order to make sound financial decisions. This elevates the level of risk and may lead to potential losses if a deal goes bad.

Nevertheless, investing in equities may not turn out to be as bad as you might think. However, I would encourage you to do your homework and stay up to date on all of the different news and information. Since we are living in the information age, it is easier now to gain access to all of the information you would need in order to guide your investment decisions.

One final note on the subject of drawbacks in the equities markets, beware of following the crows. As I stated earlier, there is a serious psychological and emotional component to investing and trading. Often, most investors will get caught up in the frenzy that may arise when a stock is "hot" or there is a great opportunity out there.

One of the axioms in trading is that if you are looking to get into a stock when it's hot, then you have already missed the boat. By the time stocks are "hot", it means that the investors who got into it at the outset are the ones who cleaned up. If you get in at the top of the wave, then you will be poised to take a hit as there is nowhere to go but down after you hit the top of the wave.

That is why it pays to do your research. Focus on the historical trends of a stock. When you see that it is significantly higher as compared to its previous low, then you might be looking at the stock being overpriced. At that point, many investors will trigger their sell points and the price of the stock will come crashing down back to its average. This is called "reverting to the mean".

Equities vs Options

So then, which is better, equities or options?

The answer to that is—it depends.

It depends on what your investment strategy is and what you are looking to achieve. So, if you are looking to put some money away for retirement and you are only concerned about saving up for the long haul, then you might not concern yourself too much with options trading. You could simply choose to buy into a mutual fund and sit back while your portfolio manager handles the dirty work.

This passive investing approach provides folks with peace of mind and assurance that they are putting their money to work. On the other hand, it doesn't provide the most attractive gains. Yet, there is always room for growth and potential to make sizeable returns over time.

Now, for more active traders, equities offer a range of alternatives from which to choose from. You can jump straight into blue-chip stocks and play it safe, or you might try to look for a hidden gem out there and try to hit a home run.

Either way, equities offer the potential for growth so long as markets don't come crashing down like they did in 1929. And even if they did, you would still have the option of finding some cheap stocks which may be poised for a rebound.

Of course, stock market crashes don't happen all that frequently (thank God), but there are market downturns which you can capitalize on. Thus, if you are looking to play the role of an active investor, you might consider day trading as an option in which you can do your best to find good deals out there and make some serious cash.

In the case of options trading, I made the point of how this is not for beginners. Options trading require investors to have some proficiency in trading before they can truly make the best of their knowledge and experience in this field.

The reason for this is that the derivatives market is highly volatile and highly speculative. So, investors need to be on their toes at all times. Otherwise, a missed opportunity could lead to taking a serious hit and losing a good chunk of change.

Also, options contracts do have a lot of legal underpinnings which most folks make not be entirely familiar with. The good thing is that once you get a good grasp of the way the contracts work, you won't have a hard time navigating the waters of the options markets. Nevertheless, it does take a bit of time and study in order to reach a point where you are comfortable with trading in options.

Furthermore, trading in options requires investors to understand the nature of the underlying assets of the contract, their pricing mechanism, and how the changes to those prices may affect the overall valuation of the contract. Consequently, a novice investor may be unfamiliar with such level of depth thereby leaving the door open to potential mistakes.

There is the possibility for investors to trade in options while maintaining a more passive role. This is generally hedge fund territory as hedge funds tend to trade in more speculative markets. In general, hedge funds are clubs of rich people who pool their money together in order to take on rather big gambles.

Hedge funds will dabble in all sorts of derivatives as these are the investment vehicles which make the most money. Therefore, hedge funds will not shy away from trading in options while enabling their investors to take on as much risk and they can bear.

Often, investors in hedge funds won't be too concerned about risk so long as they get a nice check at the end of the month.

How to Choose the Right Alternative for You

Choosing the right alternative for you boils down to your approach, be it long term or short term, and your risk tolerance.

Thus, if you have all the time in the world and are risk-averse, equities might be the best course of action for you. But, if you have more risk tolerance and don't plan on waiting for 20 years to cash in, then a more aggressive approach in the derivatives market may be the better way to go.

If you are looking to be more aggressive, then I would like to advise you to see your doctor and have your blood pressure checked out because trading in a high-risk, speculative market is not for everyone, especially those faint of heart.

So, let's consider some examples that illustrate the factors that play into making a decision on the best investment approaches.

First, let's make some assumptions.

Scenario A

In this scenario, a younger investor in their 20s is looking to get started investing money. They don't have a high-paying job and are basically starting out in life. They are simply looking to invest money while building up to buy a house, start a family, and so on. This individual investor is more risk-averse and is not keen on making any high-stakes poker bets because they are concerned with losing all their money.

So, what would be the best approach?

A safer, more diversified approach. This could be a combination of mutual funds, certificates of deposit, high-interest savings accounts, regular investment accounts, a company 401k, and government bonds.

This portfolio espouses a gradual and incremental approach as this young investor may be starting out with a couple of hundred dollars. Therefore, there isn't much they can do at the beginning of their investment career though they would have the option of building up over time.

As the investor gets older and has more money put away, they may consider more aggressive strategies such as buying into index funds or ETFs. This approach would lead to greater diversification and afford bigger returns. After 30-some-odd years of investing, the individual may be poised to have enough money put away for a comfortable retirement while having a decent quality of life.

Scenario B

In this scenario, an older investor, say in their 40s, is looking to jump into investing. They have basically paid off their house, have some money put away for their kids' college, have cars paid off, and are beginning to save up for retirement. However, saving money and having it into a mutual fund or 401k may not pay out enough for them to retirement any time soon.

So, this investor chooses to be a bit more aggressive and look for alternatives that can yield greater returns. As such, this investor may look to purchase a mortgage-backed certificate. Since this type of security is used by banks to gather funds destined for home loans, investors may find that they offer higher rates of return as opposed to the run-of-the-mill certificate of deposit. In addition, mortgage-backed certificates are generally the precursor to more speculative vehicles such as mortgage-backed securities (MBS). These MBSs were the ones that got banks in trouble back in 2008 during the sub-prime mortgage crisis. Nevertheless, those that got in on the ground floor made a killing in this type of investment vehicle.

As you can see, these are more aggressive approaches that can pay off more at the end of the day. However, you do need to be aware of what you are doing and make sure that you are not setting yourself up for a trap.

The final outcome for the investor in scenario B would be making up for lost time though there is no guarantee that this more aggressive approach may yield the results they are expecting.

Final thoughts

In this chapter, we took an extensive look at how securities can become a viable investment opportunity while options, and by extension derivatives, can provide an equally profitable opportunity though with a higher level of risk attached to them.

So, I would like to point out that it is best for you to look into all of the choices available to you so that you can make the best decision based on your personal goals when you are clear on what approach you will take.

Of course, it's always a good idea to consult with investment experts who can give you their perspective on what options are available to you. This would enable you to have realistic expectations as to what you can achieve within the timeframe you have set for yourself.

As a final thought, one of the most important traits you can exhibit as an investor is patience. While there may be the temptation to go all-in on what seems to be the deal of a lifetime, patience is what will help you stay in the game for the long haul.

So, beware of following the crowd as the crowd may be ready to fall off a cliff. As such, being smart and cautious may lead you to protect yourself a lot better than you think.

Chapter 5: Options Volatility and Greek Variables

In this chapter, we are going to drill down into the nitty-gritty of options trading and the various elements that go into the analysis of such trades.

This chapter is rooted in technical analysis, that is, the use of statistical and quantitative models to make decisions on what trade ought to be conducted and how to maximize profits. As such, technical analysis is one of the essential tools that all investors must have at their disposal.

Consequently, if investors do not have at least a basic understanding of technical analysis, they may end up making erroneous decisions due to a lack of fundamental on which to base their decisions. The most important thing to keep in mind is that as you gain more experience, you will be able to find greater value in the information and data sets provided by all the various news agencies and business intelligence units out there.

So, we will be looking at some of the most important aspects to options trading and the so-called "Greeks" that are involved in the calculation of the various operations that make up options trading.

Overview of Volatility

The first element to consider is volatility. Volatility refers to the fluctuations in the prices of assets.

As we have defined earlier, all assets, regardless of their shape, color, or size, are subject to fluctuations. Unless prices are fixed by some authority, usually the government, prices will naturally fluctuate as they become affected by market forces.

In essence, market forces boil down to supply and demand, although options don't respond the same way to market forces as equities do. Equities are a prime example of how supply and demand can affect their market price.

However, options by nature lose value over time. This is an important factor to keep in mind as the loss of value may be triggered by a depreciating underlying asset. So, the longer the option is open, the more value is lost.

Nevertheless, market volatility for options is dependent on a number of factors which don't necessarily respond to market forces in the same manner as other assets or securities.

Volatility is observed in the way prices move up and down over a period of time. These changes are tracked through averages. As such, averages provide a fairly accurate estimate of what the price of a contract or an asset is in real time.

When markets are highly volatile, there are violent swings in prices going in either direction. These violent swings may cause investors to become wary of investing in that market and decide to pull out as soon as they have a chance to do so.

When investors begin pulling out, volatility is further fueled as prices won't settle back down until they hit a trough. At that point, investors may look to get back into the market since it has hit a bottom. Nevertheless, timing the bottom of a market is very hard to do and may lead investors to lose more money before they can start to see gains.

When markets are stable, assets trade in a specific range and don't normally deviate from that range. Of course, there are peaks and valleys which may grow over time. But in general, prices remain stable thus affording investors the chance to make some positive gains even if they aren't as attractive as investors would like them to be.

Impact of Volatility on Options

Volatility is fertile ground for options.

When underlying assets in options contracts present a high degree of fluctuation, investors may seek out to purchase standard calls and puts in order to hedge their positions. As such, you might see investors purchasing calls when they feel that prices are going down and want to capitalize on a dip in the market.

On the other hand, investors may look to purchase puts when they feel the market is fluctuating and they want to get out as soon as the underlying asset hits a specific price. In this case, a given strike price, that is the price that triggers the option, can be set so that the investor can get out a specific point.

Also, volatility provides investors with the opportunity to make significant short-term gains. This can be achieved through the tried and true approach of buying low and selling high.

As volatility reaches higher levels, investors may find themselves running for cover. At this point, options underwriters may attach higher premiums to the options since market volatility may cause options underwriters to cover large margins for investors.

Consider this example:

The stock of a company is trading in a very broad range. This is due to the fact that the overall market is unstable due to mixed results from companies' quarterly earnings reports, political instability, and uncertainty in international trade.

As such, investors aren't entirely sure where to allocate their investments. So, they are pulling in and out of stocks, bonds, and so on. Now, this particular company is a large multinational player and is subject to all sorts of global conditions which may affect its overall performance.

So, investors are anticipating big news on the company's forecast for the next quarter. Since this is a large multinational player that deals with international partners, the bad outlook for the international trade market has investors worried.

Consequently, investors take out a bunch of put options on the company's stock as they anticipate bad news.

At this point, this is what is going on in the minds of investors: they are concerned that the company's earnings forecast will be lower than expected. As such, they know that as soon as news breaks, they will have to dump the stock. If and when this happens, the options which have been purchased have a strike price set as a stop-loss should the price of the stock fall below the breakeven point.

Sure enough, the news breaks and the company's earnings forecast is lower than expected. This triggers a massive selloff in that stock. The price plummets and takes a huge hit.

In this case, the investors who took out puts managed to get out before they took a sizeable hit. Those who didn't ended up going along for the ride.

Now, it's worth noting that the price of the options itself would go up in terms of the premium that investors would have had to pay in order to cover their position. This is a simple case of supply and demand.

As options underwriters see the flood in puts, they will raise the premium as they may be on the hook for a number of puts that would need to be covered at a specific point. Thus, investors may end up with having to pay a higher premium for the contract itself, that is, they will get hit with higher fees as the number of puts for that particular stock keeps climbing.

Therefore, those who got in early got a good deal, while those who got in later would end up paying the highest price.

The Black–Scholes Model

The Black–Scholes Model is used to determine the fair market value or the theoretical value of a call or put option. This model takes into account six variables which are all used as inputs in order to determine the final price of a put or call option.

The variables are:

- Volatility
- Time
- Strike price
- The type of option
- The underlying asset price
- Interest rate

When all of these variables are calculated in tandem, the result is the theoretical value of the option in question.

This model is used by options traders to purchase options which are under their calculated value and sell them at a higher price than that of the Black-Scholes Model calculation. This implies that the investor will make some money based on understanding in the option is priced below or above its theoretical value.

This model can be applied to a wide range of options such as:

- American options
- Binary options
- Cash or nothing options
- FOREX options

As such, this model offers flexibility in the way the theoretical value of an option may be calculated, thus leaving investors with the option of making investment decisions based on the results this model provides. The most important thing is that it takes volatility into account. Consequently, this helps investors determine what the best course of action would be.

Greek Strategies for Options

Throughout this book, we have talked about the Greeks. Now, we are not specifically referring to the

Greeks of lore, but rather, we are talking about a series of strategies which are named after letters in the Greek alphabet.

As such, the Greeks refer to strategies used in trading options.

In this section, we are going to take a closer look at how these Greeks work in practice.

Delta

The first of the Greeks is called "Delta".

In essence, Delta is a measure of how much the theoretical value of the option will change for every dollar the price of the underlying asset changes.

For instance, if the underlying asset is a stock which is originally valued at $10 a share, the delta of the call or put option will be the change in the options theoretical value as the price of the shares move from $10 to $11 or from $10 to $9.

The range of a Delta is from 0 to 1. Therefore, the value of a Delta will be a decimal number in that range. Also, long calls have a positive value for Delta while short calls have a negative value for Delta. Long puts have a negative Delta whereas short puts have a positive Delta.

For example, ABC Company has a price of $48, and the option has a price of $2.00 with a Delta of +0.45, and change in the price of the underlying asset, that is, from $48 to $49, will cause the options to jump to

$2.45. Conversely, if the price of the shares goes from $48 to $47, the price of the option will fall to $1.55.

As you can see in this example, the fluctuation is essentially 45 cents. In this example, we are considering the actual price of the stock and not necessarily the strike price in the option. Thus, the strike price is not taken into account, but rather, it is the asset's actual market price.

Gamma

Gamma takes the previous analysis one level deeper. So, if Delta measures the change in the price of the option as a result in the change of the price of the underlying asset, Gamma measures how much the Delta, itself, will change for every dollar in change of the underlying asset's price.

In other words, Gamma is the measure of how stable the Delta is for a given option. Thus, if there is a big move in Gamma, then the changes will be considerable in the Delta even if there is just a small move in the underlying asset's price. Also, long calls and puts have a positive Gamma, while short puts and calls have a negative Gamma.

Let's take the data from the previous example and let's throw in a Gamma of 0.07. When the price of the underlying asset moves from $48 to $49, then the Delta of the option moves up to +0.52. Also, if the price falls from $48 to $47, then the Delta becomes 0.38.

So, both Delta and Gamma move in the same direction as they both essentially measure the same thing. Thus, one change in one means a similar effect in the other and thereby affects the price of the option itself.

Theta

The next Greek is Theta. Theta, as mentioned earlier, measure the phenomenon known as time decay. Theta is an estimate of how much the theoretical value of the option falls every day that there is no shift in the price of the underlying asset or volatility.

This is a measurement of how much an option's extrinsic value is chipped away given that all elements remain constant. Furthermore, Theta can measure the difference between calls and put. This depends on the cost that carrying the underlying asset may represent. For example, if such cost is positive (the dividend paid out is less than the interest rate) then the call is higher than the put. On the contrary, if the cost is negative (the dividend yield is greater than the interest rate), then call is less than the put. Also, long calls and puts have negative Theta while short calls and puts have positive Theta.

One thing to consider is that Theta has a greater effect on those options which has a shorter expiration date than those which have a longer expiration date.

For example, an option is due in 20 days. It has a value of $3.00 and a Theta of -0.15. Every day that passes without a change in volatility or the price of the underlying asset, then the price will drop by 15 cents on the dollar. So, the next day, the option would be worth $2.85.

Now, if the option has 80 days to maturity and a Theta of -0.03, all conditions remaining equal, the option's value would fall to $2.97 and so on.

Vega

The next Greek is Vega. This is also the only Greek that doesn't have an actual Greek letter attached to it (in case you were wondering).

Vega measures how much the theoretical value of an option would change for every 1% change in volatility. This Greek is rooted in the fact that higher volatility represents higher prices for the option. On the other hand, lower volatility means lower prices in the option. Hence, the reason why Theta is time decay. When there is higher volatility, the higher the probability that the option will make money on its expiration.

Long calls and puts have positive Vega, while short calls and puts have negative Vega. Zero Vega would mean that there have been no changes in the underlying stock price.

Now, let's consider the following:

An option has a value of $2.00. It has a Vega of +0.20 and volatility is measured at 30%. In this case, we assume that volatility rises to 31%. As such, the value of the option would rise to $2.20. On the other hand, if volatility falls to 29%, then the option would be valued at $1.80.

Consequently, there is a direct correlation between the price of the option and its volatility. As stated earlier, the price of an option is higher when there is greater volatility.

Rho

This Greek is the measure of how much the theoretical value of an option would move for every 1% in change to the interest rate. This implies that the Rho for a call and put option with the same strike price and maturity would not be the same.

Rho is not commonly used in those economies in which interest rates are stable. In those economies in which interest rates are variable, then Rho plays a much larger role.

In the case of the United States, interest rates move at a rather slow pace. Since they are not quite as volatile as in other parts of the world, it is worth mentioning that a change in interest rates would lead to the recalculation of Rho, and once all models are updated, the Rho would be left alone until the next change in rates.

For instance, an option has a price of $2.00 and a Rho of +0.02 with the underlying asset's price at $48 and interest rates at 5%. Now, suppose an increase to 6% on the interest rate. That would imply a rise in the price of the option to $2.02. Likewise, if interest rates dropped to 4%, then the price of the option would also drop to $1.98.

As you can see from this discussion on Greeks (without actually speaking Greek!), the calculation of each Greek variable allows investors to predict where prices are going to fall given the changes seen in each of the outlined conditions.

Your understanding of Greeks will allow you to figure out how you can make your moves in options and come out ahead. Also, the underlying theory that supports each Greek makes it easy to see how the moves in each of the variables that make up the Black–Scholes Model provides a fairly accurate picture of the pricing for each of the options you would like to analyze.

In addition, you can purchase the software that is used by the pros to run these numbers. However, your understanding of the math will enable you to actually understand what the numbers and therefore understand what you need to do.

Historical Volatility

As mentioned earlier, volatility is the fluctuation in prices of an underlying asset in the price of an options contract.

The basic tenet is that the higher the volatility, the higher the price of the option. Conversely, the lower the level of volatility, the lower the price of the option. As such, you tend to profit more when there are wild swings in the price of underlying assets as when there is little volatility.

Therefore, historical volatility becomes the measure of volatility itself over a given period of time. Please don't think that we are going to talk about volatility over months or even years. In fact, we are not even going to talk about weeks. In the majority of cases, we are going to be looking at volatility in terms of days. This is due to the fact that higher swings in prices lead to a faster tempo in trading over far shorter periods of time such as three or four days.

As have been discussed previously, options may be purchased for a matter of days or even hours. And while there are exotic options that contain perpetuity clauses, the fact remains that most options have a very short lifespan. So, when you get into the options market, you need to think in very short periods of time.

Historical volatility can be calculated over very short periods of time such as the 2-day average of the 10-day average. Most financial news channels and other financial data subscription services will provide you with the 2-day average. This is what is commonly displayed and it tracks the trend for the asset's price over that period. Price information may be updated hourly.

The measurement of historical volatility is what feeds the calculation of the Greeks. And of course, the Greeks feed the Black-Scholes Model of option price. Thus, having a close eye on volatility is an absolute must for those who are looking to invest in options.

How to Calculate Volatility

As described in the previous section, the calculation of historical volatility boils down to the measurement in the price of the underlying asset in question.

Assuming that the underlying asset is a stock, the changes in the price of that stock would fuel its volatility. Thus, if the stock's price does not fluctuate greatly or trades within a tight range, then volatility could be considered low. But if a stock begins trading above and below its 2-day average, then you would consider that there is volatility. By the same token, if the stock starts trading well above or below its 10-day average, then you would consider that to be high volatility.

Also, as you gain more experience as an investor, you will be able to recognize volatility just by looking at prices themselves at any given time. Over time, you will become familiar with the price of a stock, for example, and recognize the range that it trades in. When you see the stock's quote above, or below that range, then you will automatically know that volatility has picked up.

Furthermore, when you hear about certain news or hear reports of certain data, you may get the sense that volatility may pick up. This is when you can pounce.

For instance, the government's job report was lower than expected for the second quarter of the year. This economic data may have a negative impact on trading within a given sector. So, investors will be looking to get out of that sector and into one which had a positive impact from the jobs report.

Consequently, volatility will pick up on as investors try to get out from one sector and into another. What this means then is that you can cash in by taking out puts and calls. Hence, if you own stock in a sector which is rumored to get hammered, you can take out puts and set a strike price at a higher point. That way, you will protect your earnings on the sale of the actual stock.

Now, you could purchase a bunch of puts for that stock, without actually purchasing the stock itself, and then as volatility begins to pick up, you can dump those puts on the investors who are looking to get out. As the volatility picks up, the price of the puts goes up and you cash in.

Sure, the shift in prices may be pennies on the dollar as we saw in the previous examples, but when you multiply pennies on the dollar over thousands and thousands of puts, you can make a good chunk of change in a very short period of time.

Of course, this is a highly speculative situation as the impact of a negative job report by the government may not impact certain sectors as expected, thereby leaving you with no gain or even a loss due to the fact that volatility didn't pick up as expected.

Implied or Projected Volatility

Implied or projected volatility is an estimation of volatility based on the historical data available for a given asset.

As we have discussed, historical volatility is measured in short periods such as days. For the sake of implied volatility, you can take the 2-day average, though it would be best to use larger data sets such as the 10-day average or the 50-day average.

The reason for this is that the 2-day average may include peaks and valleys that are due to specific events which may, or may not, be fortuitous or even bizarre. Also, there are specific events, such as reports on economic data that directly impact the volatility of a given asset. Then, as the effect of the impact wear offs, volatility reverts back to its mean.

This is something very important which you must learn to recognize. Over longer periods of time, prices develop a pattern or trend. This is nothing more than its mean which can change over time. For example, an asset's price may have an increasing mean but then a sudden change can reverse the trend. This sudden event is something you would clearly see in the 2-day average, but then would fade away back into its mean.

However, over a 10-day period, or 50-day period, not to mention its 200-day average, you would clearly see the overall trend for that asset's price. As such, it's important for you to recognize these shifts in order to make wise decisions on where volatility is heading.

Consequently, implied volatility can be seen through the analysis of the trends in an asset's price.

You can clearly define a trend just by looking at the charts though the exact numbers would have to be calculated through validated formulas.

As I mentioned earlier, you can purchase the software that can calculate this figure, though most premium subscription services would offer you this data for the price of the subscription. So, I would encourage you to take a deeper look at how implied volatility can help you understand where prices of assets are heading, and thereby help you gain a more intuitive feel for where volatility may be headed. You can also learn to recognize which important events happen throughout the year or gain a sense of how singular events may affect markets such as Presidential elections.

As I have said throughout this book, it pays to do your homework.

Diminishing Risks in Options Trading by Using Greeks

One of the core tenets that I have mentioned throughout this book is that trading in the derivatives market implies a higher degree of risk. Consequently, you need to understand such risk and find ways to protect yourself against them.

This is why the biggest risk that you can find yourself with is volatility. Volatility can zap your gains in a heartbeat and even cause you to lose money. In the worst of cases, you can lose the shirt off your back if you make a gamble on a play that doesn't work.

So, what to do?

By using Greeks, you can get a better handle of where the risk of volatility will take. For instance, if you are expecting volatility to pick up in a given period of time, you can run your simulations to determine how the theoretical price of an option would look like given certain changes in the input variables of the model.

Consequently, you can determine what price points you are looking to get into, and which price points you are looking to get out of. This is the easiest and fastest way you can protect yourself against volatility.

However, you can take specific steps toward protecting yourself in a given situation.

When you have highly volatile asset prices, you can begin by taking out options which can rid of the highly volatile asset and then bring you back in when things have settled down.

Now, let's assume volatility in each of the Greeks. In a highly volatile Delta, that is changes in the price of the asset, then you can take out stop-loss orders in order to make sure that you don't get wiped out by volatile prices.

In the case of a highly volatile Gamma, you may want to look at taking out both long and short positions on the asset itself in order to make sure that you are covered either way.

As for Theta, if you see that asset prices look to be rather steady, then you might want to consider getting out of that option position altogether and purchase the asset itself, particularly if you are looking to get out of cash. Investors who live in countries where there is a considerable risk of cash becoming devalued will look to dump cash as much as possible and move into other assets which can hold their value. This is also true of highly inflationary environments.

Regarding Vega, when you detect higher levels of volatility, this is when you need to move fast and act. So, Vega, in itself, will not derail your strategy unless you are in the midst of a financial markets meltdown. In that case, you need to dump securities right away and move into physical assets such as commodities, land, metals, and equity of privately-owned companies.

In such environments, holding on to cash may help, but if a market crash is accompanied by inflation, then cash may not be very much use. However, if you are able to react quickly, you can pick up some bargains on the cheap. This is why holding highly liquid instruments can help you get out of them quickly, take your cash and then turn around and sink it into more tangible assets, which can hold wealth over the long run meanwhile the dust settles from the crash.

Finally, changes in Rho, that is interest rates, can wreak havoc on investors. When interest rates climb, you will see the price of your options rise and then when interest rates fall, the price of option is set to go down. Bear in mind that changes in Rho may be a good moment for you to take a position since investors may panic as to the outcome of those changes in interest rates and leave them looking to see where they can turn to. When you see that Rho is going up, you can take long positions. If you see that Rho is heading down, you can take short positions. This is a good way of looking at how you can hedge your position.

Mispricing Options

Pricing derivatives is a field for skilled mathematicians comparable to putting people on the moon. If you miss by an inch, you could be hurled into space forever.

The same goes with pricing options. If you are unable to get the pricing estimations right, then when you actually close the deals, you will not be getting the price you expected. This can lead you to losing the shirt of your back, or perhaps hitting a home run by accident. Of course, the chances of hitting a home run by accident are slim. So, it pays to get pricing down right.

This entire discussion on the pricing of options leads to one thing: building accurate projections based on the input factors which affect pricing to a point where you can accurately predict where prices are going to shift. This can then lead you to wise choices on the options you can purchase or sell.

Perhaps the worst fear for options traders is to purchase options that end up going down in price or selling options which still went up in price.

In both of those cases, you would lose money by either getting less out of the deal or leaving money on the table by selling too early. So, if you are serious about options trading, I would advise you to spend some money and get the software that you need in order to run these calculations. You can purchase data packs for Microsoft Excel which can run this data for you.

One word of caution: unless you are an expert in valuating derivatives, I would highly recommend you avoid running the numbers yourself. This is why there are the software packages available for this purpose.

Predicting big shifts in options price

Predicting, also known as forecasting, is perhaps the hardest thing to do in the business world. If there is anyone who could ever get this down to an exact science, they would not only win every Nobel Prize out there, but they would instantly become the richest person in the world.

When you build the models we have discussed in this chapter, what you are doing is building a model which can help you predict the changes in asset prices, and consequently, options prices. When you get this down cold, you can accurately predict where things are headed. Sure, you may be off by a few cents here and there, but you won't find yourself out in the cold. You will always be in the ballpark.

I should warn you that options are highly speculative endeavors which may cause you to expose yourself to risk. By understanding the ways in which we can measure risk, such as through the use of Greeks, you can set yourself up for success.

So, I hope that this chapter has given you the insight that you need in order to gain a clear understanding of how you can dabble in the options market and come out a winner every time.

Chapter 6: Getting Started with Options Trading

In this chapter, we are going to cover some of the basics regarding how you can get into options trading.

The core tenet of this type of trading lies in the role you want to play, that is, being a passive investor or being a more active investor.

If you are looking to remain passive, then perhaps options may not be the right choice for you. However, if you are looking to take on a more active role, then it would be good for you to explore this investment opportunity. After all, there are opportunities for you to get into this market every day.

How to Get Started

So, there are two general ways in which you can get started.

The first is for you to open an account with a traditional investment firm and have a professional money manager handle your trades. You can specify that you want exposure to options. There you can sit down with a money manager and go over your alternatives.

This would be a good choice for passive investors who want to get exposure to this type of investment strategy but may not be keen on actually getting their hands dirty. Not all investment firms may be so accommodating with their investors. So, you would have to shop around to see which investment firm would be willing to accommodate your requests.

The second, and by far the most effective, is to open a brokerage account.

When individual investors open brokerage accounts, they tend to fall under the "day trader" umbrella. For the sake of clarity, let's define what a day trader is.

A day trader is an individual investor who, through a brokerage account, buys and sells securities, among other investment instruments, but holds no open positions at the end of the trading day. That means that these investors open their positions when the trading day starts, go through their trading day, and then close everything for the night. This is especially true on Friday evenings. Day traders would rather jump out of a plane without a parachute then leave positions open over the weekend.

Being a day trader leads to making very short-term trades, often with a window of just a few hours. This is a great way of hedging against risk, though as we have discussed, things can change in a hurry. So, it pays to be on your toes all the time.

A good rule of thumb that I live by is that if you have open positions, then you need to be at your desk. If you decide that you want to take a long lunch break, then close everything and start back up during the afternoon session. By being away from your desk with open positions, you may end up getting clobbered without even realizing it.

For those investors who are willing to keep their positions open for longer than a day, the "swing trader" category befits them. These investors or traders would benefit from keeping positions open for longer than a day since they feel that the shifts in the markets would not happen overnight, but rather may take a couple of days.

Nevertheless, swing traders don't typically hold positions open for longer than a week. That means that they will open a position on Monday morning, for instance, and close on Friday evening. This would be the longest a typical swing trader would hold an open position.

That being said, you can choose to go either way depending on the circumstance you find yourself in. If you are new to the game, I would highly recommend that you start out with day trading and gradually build yourself up to more and more complex positions.

So, once you have decided that you are going to become day or swing trader, you are ready to get started with your own account.

Brokerage accounts are offered by large investments banks and come in a wide range of colors and flavors. However, there are two main types of accounts.

- **A full-service account** – This account offers you access to the trading platform and all the analytics that come with it. All the bells and whistles in this type of account allow you to make the most informed decisions about your trades. However, they may have a high maintenance fee as all those analytics don't come free. Nevertheless, having access to all of those analytics will help you make informed decisions. Also, full-service accounts generally have a lower transaction cost. So, this is something to definitely keep in mind.

- **A discount brokerage account** – When you go the discount route, you are given access to the platform and all the trading that comes along with it, but without the bells and whistles. Therefore, you are basically on your own. You may only get access to the basic analytics, but not much beyond that. These accounts have lower maintenance fees but may also have higher transaction fees. So, you need to do your research as higher transaction fees may represent a higher cost to you especially when you make a large number of trades.

Ultimately, your choice of account lies in how comfortable you feel with your skill and knowledge about trading options.

It should be noted that you may not have access to trading options right away. You may have to build up a few successful trades before you are approved to start off with options. Or, you may have to wait a certain amount of time before you are ultimately cleared for options trading, among other derivatives such as ETFs and even futures.

Now, when you first open an account, you can get access to a practice account. This account is the real deal, but you are only doing "paper trading" that is, you are not actually playing with money.

What does that mean?

It means that if you win or lose, you won't actually be doing it with real money. Your gains and losses will be credited to an account which doesn't hold any real funds. This is a great way for you to learn the ropes of how the platform works.

Thus, doing paper trading means that you will have to invest time in learning how the platform works. In the end, though, you will be poised to start making money when you get down to the real thing.

As a matter of fact, I would encourage you to go down this road first. It will not only help you learn the ropes of how trading works, but it will also help build your confidence. This is very important since racking up losses in a simulation will not destroy your confidence as losing real money in the real thing. So, take the time to go through a practice account and learn the ropes of the trading platform you have chosen.

When you finally feel comfortable for the real thing, you can use limit order to help you keep your winnings in check.

Often, the transactions fees attached to a trade may be higher than what you actually make. So, you can use limit order to set your price for the options you are looking to purchase. When other investors hit these price points, then you can get yourself a deal. This will help you keep your profits in check.

As you gain more and more confidence, you will be able to make more successful deals. As your investable assets also grow, you will be able to make the most of your profits by reinvesting them into your account. At the end of the day, you will become more and more successful as you build momentum.

So I would encourage you to start off small and build your way up. That way, you can make the most of your investments by working through the learning curve before actually playing at the high-stakes table. Bear in mind that it is all a process. As such, you will need to take a few lumps before you really learn the ins and outs of the trading.

Buying and Selling Basics

At different points in this book you have seen me use the terms "open" and "closed" positions.

A position is when you engage in investing. If you have no investment, then you hold no position. It's not until you actually put your money to work that you actually have a position. In that regard, you have an open position when you purchase an investment. Consequently, your position is open while you hold that investment, and then it is closed when you sell it off and hold it no longer.

When you are actually trading positions, you generate a "market order". A market order is an order to buy or sell, that is, a call or put option. In general, most traders start off with "vanilla positions", that is, the standard put/call option. They don't come with any fancy add-ons and don't have any of the bells and whistles that exotic options have.

Now, with online trading, you can program your market orders so that they are triggered as soon as the strike price is hit, the maturity is reached, or you trade it manually. Whatever the condition, you can use the trading platform's automatic trading features to make your trades in real time. That way, you can track the trends in your options, but won't have to actually carry out the transaction manually. That can be done for you.

This is why I always say that you should never leave your open positions unattended.

Consider this situation:

You have placed several call options at a given strike price. When the asset hits that price, the market order is automatically generated and you have your asset. Now, let's say that you have decided to take a two-hour lunch and take a break from it all.

Fair enough, right?

Well, let's assume that your call option was one of the thousands of call options on that same asset. As such, the price spiked then other investors immediately turned around to dump their positions and cash in. Meanwhile, you were enjoying your lunch. By the time you get back, you find out what happened and realize that your asset is now under water.

You could have avoided that scenario by adding a stop-loss order to your asset so that it would trigger another put option once the asset hits the strike price you are looking to sell at. Now, depending on the platform, that may or may not be possible. For instance, you would have to take the position and then enter the stop-loss order in order to protect your position.

These are the minutiae which you need to look at when becoming familiar with your chosen platform. If you are unaware of how it all works, you could end up making a rookie mistake such as the one I have described.

So it pays to be careful with your open positions. When you exercise caution, you can take that two-hour lunch and enjoy life!

Making Sense of the Valuation of Options

In previous chapters, we had an extensive discussion on the valuation of options. Now, I don't expect you to be an expert on options valuation, at least not yet, but it certainly pays to do research and pay attention on how you can become proficient in the valuation of options.

As such, I would like to reiterate that the valuation of an option boils down to the volatility in the underlying asset. Please remember the axiom: the higher the volatility, the higher the option price. This is why volatility is now your new best friend. If you are able to make this work for you, then you will surely have a good chance to make some decent returns in the options game.

However, if you are not able to fully grasp the way options work, then I would suggest that you either seek professional financial advice or perhaps find another type of investment which you feel more comfortable with.

The legendary investor Warren Buffet once said that you need to deal with businesses you understand.

Personally, I believe this to be quite true. You cannot be truly successful at a business you don't fully understand. This is why it is important for you to make the time and effort to drill down and get to the core of your financial trading strategy. That way, when you engage in options trading, you will be able to make the most of it.

Also, when dealing with pricing, spending a few bucks on good valuation software can help you visualize where you want to go with your options strategy. Often this means having to run simulations in your computer so that you can forecast where you are going to set your positions.

That being said, it is also important for you to understand the underlying aspects to options valuation and the input factors that generate the ultimate price such as the Greeks.

I would also encourage you to make friends with like-minded individuals who have more experience than you do in the options game. They can give you pointers in the right direction and help you avoid some common pitfalls and potential dangers.

For me, it was very educational to learn from others who were more experienced than me. They helped me to see the forest for the trees. This meant that I was able to learn from their experience and also from their mistakes.

I hope that by reading this book, you are able to learn from my experience. It has taken me years to gain mastery of this topic, so now I hope that you too can learn from me.

Strategies for Buying/Selling Options

The basic strategy when it comes to trading options is to buy low and sell high. This axiom is as old as time itself.

Now, actually buying low and selling high depends on what you are doing to find those options which you can turn around and sell at a profit.

This is why the first step in the options game is for you to find good assets which you can buy low, place your options into place, and then sell when the time has come.

Of course, there are other types of options out there which you can engage in. Let's have a look at a couple of these.

Naked and covered options

A naked option is when you purchase an option for a stock or asset which you do not own. As such, you can make money when you buy low and sell high on the asset. So, if you place the option, the price falls, you purchase, and then you turn around and sell the asset before you are required to cover your position, you can make money without needing to shell out a dime.

Now, this type of transaction is risky and represents potential for disaster when the investor is required to cover the position and does not have the funds to do so. This may lead to a brokerage account being suspended.

A covered position is when you have the funds to cover a position or to purchase the asset in question.

Let's look at an example:

An investor chooses to place a call option for a stock in XYZ corporation. The investor sets a strike price of $5 per share. When the strike price is hit, then the purchase order is placed. Now, the investor does not actually have the funds to cover the position. There is a lag between the time the order is placed and the time the funds need to be delivered.

From the time the option is placed to the time the funds need to be delivered, the investor can place a put option to sell when the price reaches $5.50. When the time comes to cover their position, the investor has the proceeds from the sale to cover his earlier position.

This scheme has the potential for disaster if the time comes and the investor does not have the funds to cover their position. The put option did not go through as expected. Now, the investor needs to come up with the funds needed in order to cover such position.

Needless to say, this type of transaction is risky. That is why I always recommend investor to have some cash put away in order to cover any open positions which may lead to potential insolvency. Naturally, a consistent pattern of this type of behavior will cause investors to lose their good standing within the market and may cause their account to be suspended. In that case, the brokerage firm may require the investor to put funds down as a guarantee of good faith that they will be able to cover future positions.

Exercising options

Options can be exercised through order.

There are four main types of orders.

- **Market order**. This type of order is the main type of order. This can be a buy or sell order. All orders are market orders since they are placed in order to carry out a transaction. When the transaction goes through, the order is exercised. Market orders can be placed ahead of time, hence the option and may be canceled if the investor changes their mind based on prevailing market conditions.

- **Limit order**. This is the type of order in which the investor agrees on the price, but not the execution. As such, the order may or may not be executed. This type of order is good for novice investors in the options market. These orders are the best way to limit exposure to price volatility, both to underlying assets as well as options themselves.

- **Stop-loss order**. This type of order is placed when the investor wants to set a limit to the potential losses the investor may face due to a decline in the market conditions. So, the investor sets a strike price in which they are comfortable. The order will become converted into a put option when the strike price is triggered, the market order is then issued, and the deal goes through.

- **Stop-limit order**. This is similar to a stop-loss order. The difference is that the stop-limit order pulls the plug on the limit order when a given strike price is triggered. If such price is triggered, then the deal may still go through rather than being axed.

Advanced Options Trading Strategies

In this section, we are going to be looking at the Butterfly spread. This is an advanced options strategy that can help you make some interesting deals.

So, let's have a closer look.

The butterfly spread consists of purchasing options in 1-2-1 ratio. For instance, if the investor purchases one call option at a given strike price, and then sell two calls at a higher price. Since the investor now has an unbalanced position, the investor must now purchase a second call at the lower price in order to cover the call that was sold.

This strategy is complex since the investor is speculating with selling call options in order to avoid leaving a naked position. As such, the investor can hold one position in order to set the market order in place. When the naked position is taken on, then the investor needs to cover the back end of their position.

This implies that the investor is speculating that the second position they are covering will fall in price. Otherwise, they may lose money on the deal.

Another example of this strategy is called shorting.

In shorting a position, the investor sells calls or puts, but does not actually own any positions. When the sale goes through, the investor needs to deliver the position. At this time, the investor needs to make sure they have the means to cover that position. If the sale price ends up being lower than the purchase price, the investor will have lost on the deal.

In essence, what shorting plays off is that the massive selloff in positions will trigger a decline in the price. At that point, the investor can purchase the positions needed in order to cover the sale. Needless to say, this is highly speculative and can lead to serious complications for investors who do not have the funds or the positions to cover their shorts.

Final thoughts

Since these types of transactions tend to be highly speculative, investors should take care to ensure that they have the means to cover their positions. A worst-case scenario might be having to sell off other assets in order to cover naked positions. Therefore, uncovered positions are highly risky for investors. Thus, it is vital that you have all contingencies in place so that when the time comes to cover your positions, you are ready to do so.

Finally, it is also worth mentioning that as you become proficient in this type of trading, you can make very good gains when the market conditions are right. Of course, this requires you to keep your eyes and ears open at all time since opportunities may be right around the corner.

Chapter 7: Tips and Strategies for Options Trading

In this final chapter, we will be looking at some good tips and strategies to put into practice as part of your daily trading routine.

When engaging in options trading, the best way for you to achieve your peace of mind is to tie up all of your loose ends and ensure that you have contingencies in place, to make sure that you have everything you need to cover your positions in case anything should happen.

So, let's have a look at some tips and strategies.

Best Practices in Options Trading

The following are pieces of advice which I would like to share with you so that you can have some pointers to keep in mind in addition to all the various points we have described throughout this book.

1. When you engage in options trading, you don't necessarily need to have cash on hand in order to make deals happen. However, you will need to have enough cash in reserves in case you need to cover a position which didn't go through in time such as the case of naked options. Leaving naked or uncovered options may cause an investor to find themselves in a

tough spot and lose money on a deal that didn't work out as expected.

2. Become familiar with technical analysis. By becoming familiar with technical analysis, you will be able to engage in trading with a very good sense of where you are going and what you are doing. In addition, you will have a good sense of what to expect and what not to engage in. As such, it pays to spend a few dollars on a good analytics package or subscription which can help you stay on top of the latest information available to you.

3. Don't be afraid to get into software used for value options. Since the valuation of options can get really tricky, especially when taking all of the Greeks into account, it will be very hard for you to build your own spreadsheets and run the numbers yourself. In fact, it may take you a long time before you can actually get the handle on the proper valuation of options. Luckily, there are specialized software packages or suites for Microsoft Office which you can use to calculate and forecast the price of options. This can help you produce an accurate picture of what to

expect when you engage in these types of transactions. Furthermore, your understanding of valuation can help you get a good handle on where prices lie and if they are a good value.

4. Set limit orders especially when you are first starting out. Since limit orders agree on the price but don't hold an obligation to go through on the deal, you can be sure that you can make the deal that's right for you. In doing this, you can protect yourself from going through on a deal that may not be right for you. It also gives you the option of backing out on a deal in which circumstances have changed and may no longer be right for you.

5. Use stop-loss orders whenever possible. Stop-loss orders are a great way for you to set a strike price with which you can limit any potential losses you may face. This makes a great way of protecting your deals so that you do not, inadvertently, miss the opportunity to sell while you still make a profit or reach your breakeven point. Stop-loss orders are one of the best ways in which you can protect yourself.

Common Pitfalls to Avoid

1. Please bear in mind that when you have open positions, you need to be on top of them at all times. Often, investors feel confident when they set up all of their electronic reminders and settings in order to automate puts and calls based on strike prices and so on. Since markets are so dynamic, falling asleep at the wheel may cause you to miss out on some good opportunities especially in periods of high volatility. So, it pays to keep your eyes on the ball at all times. If you are looking to take a break, then you can close your positions and call it day.

2. Also, it's important to track your positions once you have taken them on. Options trading is not the kind of trading in which you can set an automatic timer and forget about it. If you have an open position, track it, since you may not be sure of what can happen. You can always kill orders before they are triggered. So, having a good business intelligence subscription will help you stay on top of your orders and help you make the right decisions when the time comes.

3. Another pitfall is engaging in a trade when you don't have all the information you need or when valuations look fishy. In such cases, it's better to steer clear as you may end up making a mistake by basing your decision on flawed analytics. This is especially true when you don't get the price right. In that case, if your instincts or logic tells you that the valuation of an option is off, then don't get into the deal. You may end up regretting it later.

4. It is also vital that you spend the time learning how valuations are done, but it is also important that you do not make it a regular habit of valuating every deal you make yourself. Of course, having an understanding of the underlying math and theory is essential. However, valuating deals yourself is not only time consuming but may lead to potential flaws due to human error. By using computer software designed to that extent, you can ensure that you are using the right methodology. This will enable you to double check on any valuations you see out there in the market.

5. The last pitfall I would like to point out is disregarding the Greeks. When you begin your options trading career, it's easy to overlook the Greeks. I know that it's one of the geekier parts of trading, but it shouldn't have to be. You can learn about the Greeks in a rather easy and digestible manner. I cannot stress enough the importance of making sure that you have a keen understanding of these variables so that you can truly maximize your full understanding of these indicators.

By taking these pitfalls into consideration, you will not only be able to sidestep them, but also be able to make the most of your investment opportunities. At the end of the day, you will learn as much from your own mistakes as you will from others. Of course, it is always best to learn from the mistakes of others so you can avoid making them yourself.

Getting a Handle on the Psychology of Options Trading

The final point I would like to make in this book is to beware of the psychology behind options trading.

There is a powerful psychological component that goes into trading securities, commodities, bonds, and especially derivatives.

When you engage in this type of trading, it's often easy to follow the crowd. You may even end up getting hot tips on stocks and business deals which promise amazing returns. Sure, they are out there, but by the time everyone is in on them, the ship has already sailed. When you see that all sorts of investors are flocking to a deal, it is because you are most likely getting in at the top.

What does that mean?

That there is no place to go but down.

So, always take any advice and tips you get with a grain of salt. If your judgment and intuition tell you that it's a good deal, then you can be confident that, at least of the surface, it looks good. But you should always do your homework. You have the information and the technical tools to help you follow up on these ideas and make sure that you have the right idea in place.

Also, psychology can lead people to do crazy things. The world is filled with investors who are looking to hit it out of the park. And yes, there are a few who have. But hitting a home run every time is not possible. So, you must make sure that you put a good swing on the ball when the pitch is right, and also take care of not striking out because you swung at the wrong pitch.

I know the baseball analogy may seem a bit drastic, but it is your understanding of the markets that will help you keep your cool and avoid making crazy mistakes because you got caught up in the buzz surrounding a deal.

At the end of the day, your intuition, experience, judgment, and common sense will help keep you grounded in the right opportunities which you can exploit to your benefit and that of your loved ones. After all, your gains and successes will also be those of your loved ones.

Conclusion

Well, we have made it to the end of this journey.

Indeed, options trading is an extensive topic that deserves a great deal of attention and study. You cannot expect to master this type of investment activity in a short period of time. But that doesn't mean it should take you forever either.

So, I would encourage you to do as much research as you can on this topic. In doing so, you will be building your business acumen. Since we are not born knowing everything, your understanding of these potentially complex transactions will help you gain keen insights, and thereby, an edge over other investors.

While it is true that this isn't a competition, it is a race toward your own goals. So, the faster you can get there, the better you will feel about yourself, your life, and the more you can provide for your loved ones.

Now, whether you are a brand-new investor or a seasoned veteran, I would encourage you to go back and review any of the parts in this book that you feel you need to drill down deeper on. As always, I would love to hear from you and learn more about what you have to say about the topics covered in this book. I am more than happy to provide you with some additional pointers that we didn't cover in this book.

Please bear in mind that experience is the best teacher. So, your experience in this line of business will help you gain a clear insight as to what works and what doesn't. When you reach that point, you will become so comfortable with these trades, that it will seem like you are literally making money in your sleep.

Naturally, the learning curve in trading takes time. However, this book is an attempt at flattening that curve. Therefore, you won't have to spend years going through trades, making mistakes, and learning from them. The knowledge that has been distilled in this book is precisely the result of all those mistakes made by others before us. So, I would encourage you to learn from them and build on them.

As we approach the end of this book, I have nothing more to say than thank you.

Thank you very much for getting all the way to the end of this book. I know that there are a million other things you could have been doing, and other options out there which you could have read. Yet, you read my book and that is the best validation that an author can get. I am deeply humbled by you taking the time to read my words.

As always, I would encourage you to leave a review so that others who are interested in this book will have an honest opinion about what this book is all about. Your honest opinions and comments will be very helpful to all those who are looking to engage in options trading.

So, thank you once again and happy trading!

Finally, if you found this book useful in any way, a review on Amazon is always appreciated!

The Advanced Forex Trading Guide:

Follow the Best Beginner Forex Trading Guide for Making Money Today! You'll Learn Secret Forex Market Strategies to the Fundamental Basics of Being a Currency Trader!

Neil Sharp

⊠ Copyright 2019 by _____ All rights reserved.

The follow eBook is reproduced below with the goal of providing information that is as accurate and reliable as possible. Regardless, purchasing this eBook can be seen as consent to the fact that both the publisher and the author of this book are in no way experts on the topics discussed within and that any recommendations or suggestions that are made herein are for entertainment purposes only. Professionals should be consulted as needed prior to undertaking any of the action endorsed herein.

This declaration is deemed fair and valid by both the American Bar Association and the Committee of Publishers Association and is legally binding throughout the United States.

Furthermore, the transmission, duplication or reproduction of any of the following work including specific information will be considered an illegal act irrespective of if it is done electronically or in print. This extends to creating a secondary or tertiary copy of the work or a recorded copy and is only allowed with express written consent from the Publisher. All additional right reserved.

The information in the following pages is broadly considered to be a truthful and accurate account of facts and as such any inattention, use or misuse of the information in question by the reader will render any resulting actions solely under their purview. There are no scenarios in which the publisher or the original author of this work can be in any fashion deemed liable for any hardship or damages that may befall them after undertaking information described herein.

Additionally, the information in the following pages is intended only for informational purposes and should thus be thought of as universal. As befitting its nature, it is presented without assurance regarding its prolonged validity or interim quality. Trademarks that are mentioned are done without written consent and can in no way be considered an endorsement from the trademark holder.

Table of Contents

Introduction

Congratulations on downloading this book and thank you for doing so.

The following chapters will discuss Forex trading and everything you need to learn to become a great trader. A lot of people are now earning a second stream of income through the Forex markets. If you learn how to trade Forex, then you can begin earning an attractive passive income and enjoy profits beyond what you thought possible.

Forex trading provides an excellent method of earning an additional income. This book teaches you all that you need to learn about Forex, the different currencies involved, how to buy, how to sell, and how to earn a profit. If you read all the chapters, you will understand why Forex is so profitable. In fact, the Forex market is the largest financial market in the world. Trading this market is very lucrative as long as you know what you are doing.

There are plenty of books on this subject on the market, thanks again for choosing this one! Every effort was made to ensure it is full of as much useful information as possible, please enjoy!

Chapter 1: An Introduction to Forex Trading

The term *Forex* stands for foreign exchange market and is abbreviated FX. Forex refers to the market place where different currencies are traded. A simple Forex transaction is said to take place when a person exchanges money in local currency and receives foreign currency to facilitate overseas travel. There is a huge need by people around the world to exchange currencies. Businesses and individuals trade all the time and they exchange foreign currencies in the process.

What is Forex?

The Forex market is the largest market in the entire world. It is also the most liquid financial market and generally outperforms all other financial markets in America, Europe, and all over the world. The average turnover of the Forex markets is almost $2 trillion. However, across the board, there is more than $3.2 trillion traded each day between corporations, governments, traders, and speculators. These amounts are staggering and serve as proof that the market is large enough for everyone. With such amounts at play each day, you can now understand why so many people are trading Forex on a regular basis.

There is basically no centralized platform where currencies are traded. They are traded electronically where all transactions are digitally conducted over the counter on computers spread out across the globe. Forex markets are open 24 hours a day everyday so traders can trade whenever they want and from whatever location they please.

As a trader, you stand to earn attractive returns if you engage in Forex trade. However, you need to learn as much as possible about Forex. The more you learn the better your chances of high returns. For instance, you have to understand how the Forex industry is currently mapped out. This is because market players determine how much money is available to traders. There are investment banks and hedge funds with billions of dollars available to trade while smaller traders control only a few thousand dollars.

Forex markets

The value of currencies fluctuates each and everyday. Sometimes the price is up and sometimes it is down. When we trade in currencies, we are hoping to benefit and profit from these minute but significant price movements.

One of the best known and most successful Forex traders is the billionaire George Soros. Mr. Soros made a billion dollars in a single day trading currencies. Even then Forex trading can be a risky affair and you can lose most of your money. This is the case across most financial markets so it is important to learn as much as possible about Forex trading and how to trade before starting to trade.

Technology has also improved greatly in the last couple of decades making it possible to trade online. You can now begin trading as a small trader or investor because you no longer need large amounts of money to trade the Forex markets.

As it is the Forex market is the largest financial market in the entire world. Compare its daily turnover of $3.2 trillion with that of the NYSE which is $55 billion. Even when we combine the daily output of all the world's stock markets, they only make up a quarter the size of the Forex market.

The size of the Forex market is really important. Since there are so many traders and other players, transaction costs are kept pretty low. Here are some interesting factors about Forex trading.

- Most firms in the Forex market do not charge a commission. All that you have to do is pay for the spreads.

- Since trading takes place 24 hours per day, you choose the trading times and determine how to conduct your trades

- Once you learn how to trade, you can make using leverage. This will increase your profitability immensely

- There are only limited currency pairs to choose from. This makes things easier compared to trading securities where you have over 5000 different stocks to choose from

What is traded?

Countries have their own currencies. For instance, in the US we have the US Dollar and in Canada we have the Canadian dollar. The value of any Forex currency is often a reflection of the market's opinion about the country's current and future health of the economy. Economic factors like inflation, high unemployment, and recession all have a direct effect on the strength of a sovereign currency. Forex trading therefore pits the economy of one country against that of another.

Currency pairs

Currencies are usually traded in pairs. Therefore, before trading, you will need to choose a pair to trade. The value of a particular currency against another is usually determined by the activity of the currency pairs. Take the case of the EUR or euro and the AUD or Australian dollar. When these two are paired, the movement will measure the value of euro versus that of the Australian dollar. If this value increases then it means that there has been an increase in the euro's value compared to that of the Australian dollar. The reverse is also true.

Because currencies are paired, and their values vary all the time, your aim and that of all other traders will be to benefit from the price movement.

Even small movements matter. There are several currencies that are usually paired. Basically you can pair any of the following currencies.

USD – the US Dollar
CHF – the Swiss Franc
EUR – the Euro
NZD – the New Zealand Dollar
JPY – the Japanese Yen
CAD – the Canadian Dollar
GBP – the British Pound
AUD – the Australian Dollar

The above currencies are the main Forex currencies. When you pair any of them against the US dollar, you will have a major currency pair. Examples include pairs like CAD/USD, NZD/USD and so on. Minor pairs are any pairs that do not consist of the US dollar such as CAD/AUD and so on.

Apart from the majors and minors, we also have exotic currencies. They include the Norwegian Kroner, NOK, Thai Baht, THB, South African Rand, ZAR, and the Hong Kong Dollar, HKD. An exotic currency pair is one that consists of the major currencies paired with one of the exotic currencies.

Forex trading versus Stock trading

Forex trading is vastly different from stock market trading. For starters, there is no central exchange when it comes to Forex. Traders make their trades over counters between one trader and another. They also trade through Forex dealers and brokers.

Forex traders are found all over the world. They live in different countries from Japan to China, USA and Canada, Europe and Australia, and so on. They trade across different time zones and because of this the markets are open 24 hours each working day. This is different from stock markets which are open for only a couple of hours each day.

As previously observed, currencies are traded in pairs and the prices are also quoted for currency pairs. There are regular currency fluctuations that happen frequently though in minute increments. These increments provide traders with opportunities to trade and make money off their trades. However, it is not easy to make huge returns based on small investments. This is why most traders learn how to leverage.

Advantages of Forex Trading

There are certain benefits of trading Forex compared to other forms trading. One of the main benefits of Forex trading is definitely liquidity. Forex trading is a very liquid venture and the market is also very liquid. This basically means that there are very many traders who are always buying and selling currencies. Because of this, trades are executed very fast both selling and buying hence there is always currency and profits exchanging hands. This liquidity makes the Forex market a very attractive venture for small and large investors.

Leverage

Another huge benefit of trading Forex is leverage. Most Forex brokers and agencies are often willing to lend their clients upfront money to execute trades. Leverage is basically a loan advanced to a trader by their broker. Brokers in the Forex market offer the highest leverage amounts compared to brokers in other markets.

The reason why leverage is much higher in Forex markets is because traders only require a tiny percentage of the total price of a particular position. Take a leverage of 250:1 with only $500 to invest. It is possible, using leverage, to assume a position of $125,000. If well utilized, leverage can lead to great returns.

Low entry levels

Another huge benefit of Forex trading is that entry levels are very low. This is enabled largely by the high liquidity in this particular market. Anyone with as little as $100 is able to open a brokerage account and start trading right away. This is often not the case across other financial markets where entry levels are much higher.

Low cost of transactions

Forex traders are fortunate because they are charged much lower fees by their brokers compared to other traders. The reason is because most Forex brokers usually earn their revenue via the spread. The spread refers to the difference between currency selling and buying prices. Since brokers generate their revenues from the spread and with the high volumes of trade, low fees are still profitable. This also makes it easier for most people to begin trading the markets.

Zero market manipulation

Unlike other markets, the Forex market is almost impossible to manipulate. Often in other markets such as the stocks market, some major players are able to affect prices and manipulate trade. Where markets are much smaller, a huge order from one participant or trader can largely affect prices. This is not possible on the Forex markets because this market is too large. It is 100 times larger than the New York Stock Exchange. Significant movements in Forex currencies are often as a result of government policies, reports, factors such as inflation, and global news such as war, an embargo and so on.

How exactly is Forex traded?

Trading currencies is very similar to trading stocks. In this case however, you will be buying one currency while at the same time selling another. This is the main reason why currencies are ordinarily quoted in pairs. You can have Forex quotes such as USD/AUD, EUR/JPY and so on.

Forex trading occurs instantly. This means that when you trade the trade takes place on the spot so that funds are actually exchanged instantly. Keep in mind that you are basically buying a currency while selling another all at the same time. As an example, if you see the EUR/USD Forex quoted as 1.19, this means that you need to pay $1.19 in order to buy a single euro.

Therefore, as you trade currencies you will actually be selling your dollars and use the proceeds to purchase Euros as in our case above. Also, each currency has a certain interest rate attached to it by its Central Bank.

Even then, you need not be a regular trader in order to benefit from the Forex market. Simply travelling overseas or buying products from another country will have you participate in Forex trade.

Carry trade

Another method of making money while trading currencies is carry trade. This method is popular among currency traders. It is basically a strategy where a trader borrows low-interest currencies and then uses these to invest in high-interest currencies. The aim of this approach is to earn a profit from currency trade and also hope the currency purchased will appreciate in value.

For success with carry trade you should focus both on pairing a high interest currency with a low interest one and the spread's direction. The ideal situation should be where the central bank of the currency in which you have a long outlook is seeking to increase interest rates whereas the other is expecting lower interest rates.

In brief, the aim in this instance is to identify a currency pair whose interest spread is high and is experiencing an upward trend. To implement this strategy successfully, you will require a deeper understanding of fundamentals that affect interest rates.

Eight major currencies

In the stock market, you get to choose from thousands of different stocks. However, in the Forex markets, you get to choose from only 8 major currencies which represent eight major economies of the world. These include Canada, EU, Australia, United States, Japan, New Zealand, the UK, and Switzerland.

These eight nations have some of the world's most sophisticated financial systems. When you focus mostly on these eight currencies, you can financially benefit from the currency fluctuations that happen all the time. You will also earn from the world's most liquid and creditworthy financial market.

As a trader or investor, you can access financial and economic information from any of these countries on a daily basis. This information can be used for analysis so that you can determine the best currency pair to choose from. As such, you are able to trade currencies based on sound and trustworthy information and analysis.

Interest rates

As you begin trading in currencies, you need to know that there is interest charged by various central banks. When you deal in any currency, you will be obligated to pay some interest on the currency.

Basically, you make a profit on the currency that you buy but pay interest after selling a currency.

As a trader, it is crucial that you find out the direction of interest rates. Of course there are certain factors that determine this. One of these is the size of a country's economy. Country's that register strong growth and whose economies are performing well are likely to raise interest rates in the course of the financial year.

On the other hand, countries whose economies are experiencing difficulties and performing poorly are likely to experience reduced interest rates. If you can understand how interest rates work and how they affect currencies and other related policies, then you stand a good chance of success trading currencies.

Another important point to note is that there is plenty of leverage that you can use to your benefit. Leverage sometimes gets as high as 100:1 which implies that with only $100 you can handle currencies worth a whooping $10,000. If you are an astute trader, then you can earn that much money with only $100.

A lot of successful Forex traders use leverage to earn huge profits with limited resources. You should however avoid leverage as much as possible until you have sufficient experience trading currencies as well as an understanding as to how it works.

There is some risk involved

You also need to be fully conscious of possible risks when trading currencies. This is true not just with Forex trading but with all kinds of trades because there is some risk involved. What you need to do is get some education about Forex trading, learn how to do it properly and then do a lot of practice on a demo platform. It is only through practice and understanding how Forex works that you will be able to trade safely and make attractive profits.

Chapter 2: The Basics of Trading Forex

Forex trading has become extremely popular as it provides a pathway for any keen trader to join and begin earning huge profits. Currencies are crucial to the global economy and as such are held to a certain level of importance. The reason is that they are used to facilitate foreign trade, business, travel, and much more.

There is no central exchange platform or marketplace where Forex trades are managed or overseen. Most trades are conducted and concluded on digital platforms across the internet and sometimes over the counter or OTC. As such, all trades are executed over computer networks across the entire globe.

Forex markets are available 24 hours a day, Mondays to Fridays. Traders have to sign up with a Forex brokerage firm so as to trade. They provide their services at these times. Trades occur across all the different time zones and in all major financial capitals including Sydney, Tokyo, Singapore, Paris, Zurich, New York, and London.

Forex Trading Strategies and Styles

Now that you understand the basics of Forex trade, you need to learn how to trade. There are different strategies that you can adapt when it comes to Forex. Some of these strategies and approaches are thought to be a lot more effective in comparison to others. Once you learn about these strategies, you should try them out in order to identify the one that suits you most and that you are most comfortable with.

First of all, you will come across bid and ask prices on Forex platforms. The bid price simply refers to the value or cost of a currency that you want to buy. Therefore, when you buy a currency, you will be paying the bid price. On the other hand we have the ask price. The ask price is the price at which you will sell your currency. These prices are constantly fluctuating based on the demand and supply in the market just like it happens on other markets.

- *Day trading strategy:* This is a strategy where trades are entered into and then concluded within the same day. If you set up a Forex trade via this strategy, then you will conclude it before the end of the day. The main aim of this strategy is to protect a trader from incurring overnight losses as there are events that could alter price directions of certain currencies.

- *Swing trade strategy:* This is a trading strategy that lasts between a single day and an entire week. You adapt this strategy if you have a long term outlook on certain currencies and wish to allow the strategy to mature.

- *Trading the trend strategy:* In this instance, a trader will be trading in accordance with the market trend. As such, you will follow the market trend and trade according to its movement.

There are other strategies that you can use as well. These include technical trading, intraday trading, fundamental trading, as well as position trading. Try out as many of these strategies and then identify that works out for you and fits your needs.

Currency Pairs

Now keep in mind that Forex currency is always traded in pairs. What this simply means is that two currencies are paired together and the price of one is quoted in reference to the other. As such, these currency pairs are essential components of currency trade. Also, the prices of the currencies keep changing all the time depending on a number of factors.

Earlier we had mentioned that currencies are classified as the majors, the minor ones, and the exotic currencies. The majors include the currencies of the US, Canada, UK, and European Union. These are among some of the worlds' largest economies. A major is a currency pair that includes the US dollar. Examples include EUR/USD, AUD/USD and JPY/USD. Minors are currency pairs that do not include the US dollar. For instance, JPY/EUR, AUD/NZD and so on are considered minor pairs. Exotic currencies are currencies that do not belong to major world economies. They include the Hong Kong Dollar, Norwegian Kroner, and the Russian Rubble among others.

We also refer to the pricing and quotation structure of currencies as a currency pair. When you choose your preferred currency pairs, you will then proceed to trade these at the Forex markets. You will be simultaneously buying one currency and at the same time selling another. Even then, traders often view currency pairs as a single entity that can be used for trading purposes.

Example

Let us take the example where we have the Euro and US dollar paired together. Hence our currency pair in this instance is the EUR/USD. In this case, we refer to the EUR as the quote currency while the USD is referred to as the base currency. In our case above, the value of the currency pair will simply imply the value of the quote currency needed so as to buy a single unit of the base.

Therefore, the ask price simply refers to the price of selling a particular currency pair while the bid price refers to cost or price of purchasing a currency pair. When you are in the Forex market buying a currency of a particular trade, then you will be said to have taken a long position. In this instance, you will be hoping that the price will rise higher until such a time as when you are ready to sell. You will then sell at an attractive and worthwhile profit.

In some instances, you may need to get to the Forex market to sell your currency pairs. When you do this, you will be entering a short position and hoping to sell your currencies for a tidy profit. You will make a profit in this instance which will be the difference between the price at which you bought currencies and the selling price.

Base currencies versus quoted currencies

As you deal in Forex currencies, you will be purchasing the base currency then selling the quoted currency. The reverse is true when selling a currency pair. In this case you will offer buyers the base currency and in return you will get paid the quoted currency.

Essential Forex Terminology

The Forex market comes with its own unique jargon and terms. In order to understand what is happening at the markets, you should learn the jargon used by other traders and players in the Forex market. Before you begin trading currencies you will have to understand some basic terminology. These terms pertain to the Forex market and will enable you to understand and interpret different calculations and Forex quotes. It is essential to learn some of these terms so that you become an able and capable trader.

- **Cross rate:** This term refers to the exchange rate between two different currencies. In most cases, these currencies are usually not the main currencies of the country where the quotes are issued. The term is sometimes used to refer to currencies that are not paired with the US dollar.

  As an example, consider the situation where a currency pair including the British Pound and the New Zealand dollar is quoted in a Canadian magazine. This currency pair can be referred to as a cross rate. However, if the currency pair involved the US dollar, then it would not be a cross rate.

  Leverage: In Forex trading, the term leverage refers to the provision to control a huge sum of money in the markets. Most Forex trading

Using leverage, you can make pretty attractive returns from your trades especially because of the small and minute movements that regularly occur on the trading platform. You need to be extremely cautious, however, when you use leverage because even though you stand to make astronomical profits, you also stand to lose huge amounts of money.

Exchange rate: This refers to the actual value of a single currency when it is expressed in terms of a different currency. As an example, if we have USD/CAD as 1.2800, this means that 1 USD is equivalent to CAD 1.2800.

Spread: Any quote will have a bid and offer price or the buy and sell quotes. The difference between these prices is what is known as spread. As an example, if we have a USD/CAD quote expressed as 1.2800/02, then the spread in this case is equal to the difference between 1.2800 and 1.2802. This difference is read as 2 pips.

Pips: The term pip is very common when it comes to Forex trade. It simply refers to the difference between the values of two currencies. Therefore, when you have a currency at $1.1200 and another at $1.1250, then the difference between the two is referred to as 50 pips.

Pip actually refers to the last decimal position on a currency pair quotation. They are often used when traders use either two or four decimal places in their quotes. Pips are sometimes referred to as points or a point. In generally, a pip is simply the tiniest increment in the price movement of a currency.

Margin: When you begin trading, you will be required to deposit a certain amount into your trading account by your broker. This is the amount that you will use to trade. It is also the amount where any fees and costs will be charged. Therefore, the deposit that is needed to maintain a position is basically known as the margin.

Margin amount can be either used or free. A free margin is an amount that is required to open a new position in the Forex markets while a used margin is one that is necessary to maintain an already open position. Let us assume that you have about $1000 in your trading account and need 1% in order to open a position in the market. This basically means that you deal in a position that is worth a total of $100,000.

A margin call can be made by a broker when an account drops to levels that are below the amounts needed to hold open positions. Therefore, when your accounts fall below the minimum amount, you can expect a margin call from your broker. In some cases, the broker will close the trade should the amount available be less than that required. Sometimes brokers set the limit which is often about 50% of the amount needed to open a trade.

Hedging: This term refers to a new position being opened by a trader but in the opposite direction. When you open a new position that is directly opposite a current position, you will be said to have taken a hedging position. This is especially when trading the same currency pairs. For instance, if you wish to hedge a 0.2 buy position on the

CAD/NZD, then all you need to do is to open a 0.2 sell position on the same currency pair. When you hedge a position, you will not require additional margin.

Swaps or Rollovers: Sometimes Forex traders get a chance to not just earn profits but also to make capital gains. When we trade currency pairs, we also involve two varying interest rates. Sometimes you will not just make a profit from trading interests but also from an increase in interest rates.

Should the rates increase, then you will earn what is known as a rollover or interest. Sometimes the interest rate may fall. In this case, you will have a negative rollover. When the rollovers are positive, they will add to your profits. However, when they are negative, your trades may incur additional costs.

Commissions: Traders have to pay fees, charges, and commissions to their brokers. The fees and commissions will vary from broker to broker based on certain factors.

Nicknames for most major Forex pairs

Most major currencies traded on the Forex markets have certain nicknames attached to them. These make it easier for traders and others in the sector to easily identify them. Here are some of the common terms used to refer to major currency combinations.

1. EUR/USD – the Euro
2. AUD/USD – Aussie dollar
3. GBP/ USD – Sterling or Cable
4. USD/JPY - Dollar Yen
5. NZD/USD – Kiwi
6. USD/CHF – Swissy
7. USD/CAD – Dollar Canada

How to read Forex quotes

If you intend to trade the Forex markets and make a profit, then you will need to lean how to accurately read currency quotes. This is necessary before you begin trading. As we have already seen previously, currencies are paired together in Forex.

You will notice that foreign currencies are often quoted in pairs. This is because we are expressing the value of one currency using the other. You can also view this is as selling one currency while simultaneously buying another. Let us look at an example of a quote.

USD/AUD = 1.2800

The USD component in the above quote is referred to as the base currency while the AUD component is referred to as the quote currency. The quote currency is also known as the counter.

When you purchase a currency pair, then the quoted exchange rate will reveal the amount of the quoted currency needed to purchase the base currency. For instance, in the above the example, you will need to pay 1.2800 Australian dollars to purchase 1 US dollar. On the other hand, if you were to sell one US dollar, you will receive 1.2800 Australian dollars.

The Bid and Ask Prices

Ask price – the ask price is basically at which you buy a particular currency pair. It is the price at which your broker or the market is willing to sell you a specific currency pair. The ask price basically allows you to purchase a single unit of your base currency.

Bid price – this is the price at which you will sell your currency pair. It is also the price at which the market, or your broker, is willing to purchase currencies from you. The bid price is the price at which you will sell a single unit of the base currency.

Bid/Ask spread: The bid/ask spread is simply the difference between ask and the bid prices. Spreads often varies from one broker to another.

Chapter 3: Forex Trading Strategies

Now that you have learned the basics of Forex trading, it is time now to delve deeper and learn about actual trading strategies. Trading strategies can be termed as techniques used by traders to enable them decide whether to sell or buy a currency pair at a specific time.

Fundamental and Technical Analysis

When applying Forex trading strategies, we use outcomes of either fundamental analysis or technical analysis. Therefore, before you start trading, you mush conduct some analysis so as to know the best currency pairs to sell or buy and the most appropriate time to do so. Apart from the outcome of the analysis, a strategy should also include trading signals.

However, you do not always have to conduct the analysis yourself if you do not want to even though it is highly recommended. There are experts who do this on behalf of others and provide outcomes online. You can find analysis on the internet which you can then use for your trading strategy.

Discipline

One of the most important aspects of a good trading strategy is that it should first and foremost be well thought out and back-tested. This means that the strategy should be proven to work well even after implementation. As such, you should implement the strategy once you are ready and then stick with it. You should not change your mind mid-way but stick with a strategy to the end.

As a trader, you will require self-discipline. This is the only route to success. All too often, young or novice traders enter a trade by implementing a strategy then begin to panic shortly thereafter. When you let emotions lead you, then you will never make any profits and will lose money. This is because emotions will lead you to think that you are losing money. Instead, be disciplined and stick to a strategy. Let the strategy run its course just as long as you implement it correctly and follow it as required.

Putting together a strategy

Trading strategies for Forex traders can be automated or manual. These are used to generate trading signals. Manual systems require that you sit on a computer and find the signals then determine whether or not you should buy. On the other hand we have automated systems. These require the trader to develop a suitable algorithm that identifies trade signals and then executes them all on its own. This is a preferred approach basically because it eliminates the emotion out of the trade. This way, you get to improve your performance. It is advisable to take caution when buying strategies from different places online. This is because it is rather difficult to track down the performance of these strategies. A lot of successful trading systems are never revealed to the public. You will also need to make a determination about the currency pairs you wish to trade. Once you do, you should then work to become an expert at studying the specific currency pair.

Most of the times when traders speak of Forex strategies they usually refer to particular methods that can be applied to trades. However, these often are just an aspect of a total plan. A strategy will mostly point you towards a favorable entry point. This is the best point at which you should enter the market. However, apart from these, you should also consider other aspects. These include the following;

- Most favorable entry points
- Position sizing
- Best exit points
- Risk management techniques
- Trading tactics

There are a number of trading strategies out there so choosing the best and most profitable is crucial. A good strategy can be one that appeals to you as an individual. It should be one that you are comfortable and happy with. Only if this is the case will you thrive and become profitable. If you try some other strategy simply because it worked for someone else, then this will probably not work out. Basically what works out for someone else may not necessarily work out for you. This is why you need to practice a lot and try out as many different strategies as possible. Only then will you find out the strategy that best matches your personality.

On the other hand, it is very possible as well, that a strategy that worked out for someone else also works out for you. At this stage, the key is as much practice on demo platforms as possible and learning self-disciplined. If you learn from the onset to be a disciplined trader then you will definitely be on your way to success. A disciplined trader is one who spends time identifying a suitable strategy then sticks with their strategy to the end.

As a trader, you should set up a trading system on platforms such as Meta Trader. On this platform, you are able to automate your trading instructions. This way, you will first come up with a strategy, develop the appropriate execution technologies. When you automate a trade and put a stop loss measure as well as take profit point, you should comfortably let the trade take its course. When you use a platform such as Meta Trader, you will also be able to perform a back test just to confirm how your strategy will play out in the real market.

Trading styles

There are a number of very popular trading styles adapted by traders around the world. These strategies range from short to long-time frames. They have been successfully implemented over the years and are still popular even today. As a Forex trader, you need to be aware of the various strategies and styles for successful trading. This way, you can always navigate from one trading style to another should you feel that there is one not particularly working for you.

1. *Day trading:* When you execute day trading strategy, you will have to exit a trade before the close of the day. This means that you enter a trade in the morning or sometime during the day and exit before the day ends. As a beginner, this strategy can be one of the best because it saves you from any shocks or losses that may occur during the night. Day trades usually last only a couple of hours. This way, you are able to enter a trade after doing your analysis, rake in some profits, and then exit when you can. A suitable example of day trading strategy is the 50-pips.

2. *Scalping:* Scalping is a trading strategy that lasts a very short period of time. You simply enter a position on the Forex markets and shortly thereafter you exit and collect your profits. The aim of this strategy is to try and beat the bid-offer spread and then make a modest profit before exiting the trade. Scalping makes use of tick charts so you know exactly when to enter and at what point you should exit a trade. You should also ensure that you make use of scalping indicators provide via tools which are readily available to you.

3. *Position trading:* This is a strategy where a trader follows the trend. It is a long term strategy with the aim of maximizing profitability especially in

instances where there are huge price movements. When you adapt this approach, you will mostly be inspecting end-of-day charts. You will also need to be a rather patient investor with a deep understanding of market fundamentals.

4. *Swing trading:* A trader using this approach will basically hold a position for a couple of days. This time period is often between a single day and an entire week even though this period can sometimes extend into weeks and months. As a swing trader, you will typically inspect charts in thirty-minute intervals.

Additional Forex Trading Strategies

50 Pips per Day

This is a Forex trading strategy that seeks to benefit from early market movement especially of very liquid currencies. The most liquid currencies are the USD, GBP, and the EUR. These are the best to deal in and the most ideal especially for this particular strategy.

Often on early mornings, different Forex traders place dual positions and sometimes two pending orders. As soon as one of these positions is activated through price movement, the other position gets cancelled immediately.

This strategy targets a profit of 50 pips and has a stop-loss order ranging between 6 and 10 pips. This stop-loss order is often placed below or above the 07.00 candlestick GMT time. Stop-loss orders are placed to prevent losses. When your position in the market starts to lose money, it will only do so to a pre-determined point before automatically exiting. Exiting a position at a predetermined point helps prevent further losses. Risk management is essential in this case because this approach is highly risky.

Daily charts strategy

A lot of experienced Forex traders prefer trading the daily charts instead of other strategies such as the short-term ones. Daily charts have less market noise compared to others such as the Forex 1-hour charts and others with lower timeframes. Using the daily charts can enable you gain over 100 pips each day since they come with longer timeframes.

Also, daily charts provide signals that are a lot more reliable compared to other signals and chances of earning a huge profit are much better. There is also no need for fundamental analysis or worries regarding random price changes or daily news. There are however 3 main factors that affect this trade.

1. *Identify the trend:* You first need to identify the trend. This is crucial because markets first trend and then consolidate. This is a process that repeats over and over so be on the lookout for the trend.

A reliable way of locating the trend is to study prior Forex data for approximately 180 periods. This data will enable you identify upswings and downswings as well. When you do this, you will easily be able to identify the trend.

2. *Remain focused:* As a trader, you need to be patient and allow trades to take their course. You need to be able to manage the urge of exiting trades prematurely. This calls for discipline and focus. Stay focused on current trade and trust that your analysis is correct.

3. *Make use of large stop losses and less leverage:* You need to be on the lookout for the occasional intraday

swings which can sometimes be quite large. The best approach to mitigate these large swings is to use stops that are sufficiently large.

Trend-following Strategies

Markets always set a trend then follow this trend for a considerable time. However, sometimes the trend tends to experience sharp price spikes which could head up or down. This is often as a result of volatility. In other situations, the market may move outside the range. It may then trend above the line of resistance or below the support line so that a new trend actually starts. When the trend moves below the support line, then traders begin to keep off. The reason is that more and more low prices get established. This means opportunities are being created to allow them to enter trades at much cheaper prices. Traders often wait until the trend bottoms out. At the same time there could be traders who begin to panic and sell their currencies as fast as possible.

However, the trend continues until the price settles down without the risk of further downward spiral. Buying when the currency prices are down and selling at higher price is the aim of Forex traders.

This way you will be able to make a tidy profit in the end. Traders often feel encouraged to purchase currency pairs in the open market once the trend breaks through the resistance.

In some instances trends tend to be prolonged and even dramatic. Since there is plenty of movement in the markets, the trend is often thought of as the best Forex strategy especially for beginners. Forex trading systems that follow the market trend use indicators that alert traders whenever new trends set in even though there is no sure way of determining this.

Positive outlook

Now when signal indicators point to a specific time when a trend started, then the odds will swing in your favor. A breakout is the instance where we notice a trend that is just about to begin. Systems that follow the trend need traders with a specific mindset because you can lose profits should the markets experience a sudden swing. As such you really need to be mentally strong and psychologically prepared for such an eventuality.

The 4-Hour Trading Strategy

There is yet another profitable and beneficial strategy that you can consider using. This is the 4-hour trend strategy which is more suitable for the swing trader. Traders use the 4-hour charts to find signals that indicate the best market entry points. You also need to use the 1-hour charts in order to determine or confirm the exact position to assume in the Forex market.

Counter – Trend Strategy

We also have the counter-trend strategy. This is a strategy that counts on the fact that any breakout trends never end up as long-term trends but will fizzle out eventually. It is crucial to observe that this approach does require strict risk management. There is a good reason for this. For instance, the strategy basically relies on resistance and support levels remaining firm. Should they fail and instances such as large downsides occur, then potential losses will be significant.

As a trader, you will need to monitor the markets constantly. This regular monitoring will help to keep your account safe. For the best outcome, you will need to be in a volatile yet stable market. Such an environment is crucial as it offers attractive price swings which are managed within a range.

You need to be aware that the status of a market can change without much warning. An otherwise quiet and stable market can begin to trend then experience volatility before calm returns. These changes are often unpredictable and uncertain. Therefore always examine the state of the market before choosing to enter.

Technical indicators

There are certain things that will assist with your strategy. These are technical indicators. A lot of these indicators have been developed in the recent past. They provide crucial information that you need as a trader if you are to execute trades successfully.

In all, the best and most preferred Forex strategies are those that are well-established, simple, and easy to understand. These strategies have worked for numerous traders over the years and have helped produce some of the best traders in the market today. You need to a lot of practice using demo accounts and try trading using different strategies. It is only through such practice that you will be able to determine which specific strategy works best for you.

Best Indicators for Forex Trading

When you begin trading Forex, you will be successful if you follow the path that many others have in the past. You first need to know how to trade. This is crucial. To trade successfully, you will need to make use of trade indicators and specifically technical indicators for the Forex market.

Technical Indicators

Technical indicators are simply tools of a mathematical nature that you use to analyze factors pertaining to Forex trading. These factors are open and closing prices, volumes, high and low. The indicators, once calculated, are plotted on graphs which can then be read and interpreted. These graphs are referred to as chart patterns. To be a successful trader, you will need to learn how to read charts.

Most of the current technical indicators were actually designed for daily charts and the stock market. The reason is because back then charts were only updated for a maximum 24-hour period. This was many years before the internet was created. There are different types of indicators that you can use. These include the following;

- Trend indicators
- Volume indicators
- Momentum indicators
- Volatility indicators

Changing a Forex Trading Strategy

Basically when you implement a strategy it should work out well for you. However, a strategy is only effective if you follow all the rules. Most traders find this to be true whenever they implement a strategy. In rare cases though some strategies simply do not work and they may need to be changed.

A strategy that is effective today may not necessarily be a successful strategy tomorrow. In short, any strategy that does not make you money, is not producing results and is not profitable can be changed. But before changing your strategy you should consider the following measures.

1. Try and match trading style with risk management: Examine the risk versus reward ratio and determine if it is working. If it is unsuitable at this point, then you may want to change the strategy and adapt one that actually works for you.

2. Understanding a strategy: Sometimes traders really do not grasp a strategy. Failure to fully comprehend a strategy may lead to failure and the strategy basically wont work. This calls for changing strategy to one that the trader comprehends.

3. Changing market conditions: Some strategies depend on certain market conditions. If you implement a strategy that heavily relies on conditions in the market, then changing conditions may affect the strategy. In this case, you may need to adjust you strategy and find one that works for the prevailing market conditions.

While a change of strategy is recommended in some instances, it can sometimes prove to be costly. Try not to modify your strategies too often and instead trust your analysis and back-testing. If not then you stand to lose out immensely. Here are some key points to note.

- A Forex strategy is simply a trading technique used for trading currencies and generating profits in the Forex market

- You will often need to use certain tools to support and guide your trading strategy. These tools are often digital even though there are manual ones

- Before implementing any strategy, you should first back-test it and then implement it on a demo platform. Allow it to run before eventually implementing it live on the markets.

As an example, a novice trader first determines that the USD/JPY is a currency with plenty of potential and he foresees it doing well in the near future. Before trading though he performs his technical analysis. Using one of the moving averages he determines a trend in the market. The trader then goes ahead to trade the USD/JPY currency pair and make some attractive returns in the process.

Essential Things to Make you a Successful Forex Trader

As it is, there is not one single strategy of formula for success trading the Forex market. A great way to view Forex trading is to view the markets as the ocean and traders are the surfers. Surfing is a sport that requires skills. The more you practice the more your skill improves. Also, to be a great surfer, you need certain tools such as proper surfing board, swimming kit, and so on. Other essentials include proper balance, talent, discipline, and being comfortable in the deep sea.

If you had a great fear of deep waters or lacked proper balance then you would not make a great surfer. The same is true when it comes to Forex trading. You need to have all the essential ingredients if you are to succeed and be profitable. If you do not have the necessary tools and skills then you should not enter the water and surf the waves. Similarly, avoid the Forex market until you learn how to trade and become profitable.

To become a successful trader you need to have proper analytical skills, the necessary tools, and proper implementation techniques. All these essential skills and techniques are summarized below.

1. Your approach to Forex

One of the most important things you need to do before you begin trading is to prepare as much as possible. Proper preparation is key to successful Forex trading. Think about your personal aims and your temperament and persona. If you really understand Forex, then you will do better in that market. however, if you feel inclined towards something else such as stocks or futures, then pause and think things over.

2. Time frame

When you want to start trading, think about the timeframes involved. This is because there are different strategies and most vary with time. There are 5-minute charts, day trading, swing trading, and so on. Are you comfortable holding overnight positions? You should also consider incurring losses on days when trades do not work in your favor.

Think about your lifestyle. Are you busy and wish to trade Forex in your spare time? Then think about trading evenings only. Also, are you intending to start trading as a full time occupation? Then there are strategies that allow you to do this. Think about day trading for instance. You can enter the markets, watch your screen all day and exit at day's end. It's crucial though to keep in mind that you can make huge profits trading the Forex markets but success comes with time and not overnight.

3. Trading attitude

Your trading attitude is closely related to your behavior. As such, your behavior will have a huge impact on certain characteristics. These include discipline, patience, realistic expectations and objectivity. Discipline is the choice and ability to be patient and let a trade run its course.

There will be occasion when the price action will not get to your expected price level. When this happens, your first instinct would be to pull away from the markets to avoid losses. However, this is not a smart approach and you should stick to your plan. Trust the systems in place to work in your favor. However, should your stop loss management system ask you to pull out of the market then you should do so without hesitating.

Objectivity here refers to emotional detachment. You need to be able to eliminate all forms of emotion from your trades. Emotional trade is a weakness that many novices exhibit. They notice the first sign of losses and choose to exit for fear of losing their money.

4. Implementing a Forex strategy

Experts have already demonstrated that there is absolutely nothing like a profitable trade only. This is because even the best and most seasoned Forex traders lose money. Profitability is found in proper execution of trades and risk management techniques used.

Eventually, everything will boil down to your risk management and control. To achieve risk management successfully, you will need to ensure that your strategy starts of in the correct direction. Keep watching the performance of your trade and the system in place. Should any adjustments be necessary then make them as early as possible. You will probably get your direction right after the second or third attempt.

In conclusion, we can conclude that Forex trading is as much an art as it a science. This means you need multiple skills as well as proper state of mind to succeed. You will either make or lose money depending on how you apply your techniques and according to your discipline. You can always take small losses as these are part of being a trader. Take these quickly so as to avoid the larger more devastating loss.

Chapter 4: Best Trade Entry and Exit Strategies

Trade entries are a huge determinant of whether your trades will be successful or not. Most traders tend to take entry points for granted and focus their energies on the actual trade. A shift from this approach towards application of the best trade entry strategies will significantly improve the risk-reward potential of any trade and also helps you to achieve a superior stop loss location.

As a trader, one of the most essential aspects you need to focus on is establishing if there is a trend in the market or not. Ordinarily, you would simply need to trade with the trend setup or consider setting up a countertrend reversal setup.

It is crucial that you learn how to determine the best Forex entry methods and the essential tools you require for market entry. There are a couple of different methods that you can use to successfully enter the market. If practiced consistently, they will enable you become a more proficient trader.

1. Assess the Market

As a Forex trader, you need to recognize the environment in which the market is operating. By identifying the operating environment, you will then be able to establish the most appropriate strategies and tactics at any given time. You need to determine what kind of market structure you would like to trade and what type of trades you wish to make.

2. Scan your Charts

Among the first things you need to do before the start of your trading day is to scan your charts. You should first determine the best Forex pairs to trade then scan the charts. One of the best approaches is to scan the markets right after the closure of New York and the opening of European markets. During these hours, the market action goes down after the previous trading day.

Even as you scan the charts, be on the lookout for price action, levels, and trends. It is important to look out for a trend. For instance, watch out for any patterns that involve low highs and low lows or higher highs and higher lows. Also be on the lookout for the direction of the 21 and 8 daily EMAs.

3. Establish a Trend

You should endeavor to establish a trend. It all comes down to looking for the higher highs and higher lows versus the lower lows and lower highs. If you can establish a crystal clear trend, then it will be worth much more than gold. Successful traders always trade along a trend and rarely against it.

4. Try and Set Up Trades at the End of Each Day

This is a very easy yet very effective approach. If you can set up your trade at the close of New York markets, then you will have an effective start. You will also eliminate any mental confusion and noise brought on by use of intraday charts. You should ensure that you monitor all your trades once or twice each trading day in order not to unnecessarily fiddle with the trades. This will also help to eliminate the psychological aspect of trading.

As a trader, you either specialize in one type of trading or are a master in several types and can choose a preferred type depending on market situation. It is important to keep this in mind when building your strategy. For a trader who has mastered different trading styles, the best approach is to focus on only a few currencies while a specialized trader should focus on scanning the market and viewing more Forex currency pairs.

Scanning the Market

When scanning the markets, the aim is to look for the following;

- Price action
- Trends
- Levels

What you need to determine first is whether there is a trend in the market. This is ideally not a science but actually an art. Patterns of high highs and low lows are crucial at this stage because they point to a trend.

Get Better Prices with Limiting Orders

A limiting order is also known as a pending order. It is placed above or below the prevailing market price depending on the direction of the trade. Limiting orders provide you with the ability to enter a trade at a price of your choosing. The only challenge is that you may not always get into a trade at all.

If you are trading short, the limiting order should be set just above the prevailing market price. However, if you are trading long, then the limiting order should be placed below the prevailing market price. Here is how to apply the limiting order.

1. **The Trade Entry Tip:** This is where a trader enters a price action signal on a 50% retrace. It simply means that you enter a limited order where the price retraces back to the 50% level of a pin bar. This approach greatly improves your risk vs. reward ratio and it allows you to place a tighter stop loss. You will easily be able to double your returns.

Another benefit of this approach is that you have more flexibility regarding where you place or locate your stop loss. You can choose the normal distance stop loss or enter a trade with a much tighter stop loss. You get more breathing space within your trades as a trader when you use a regular stop loss distance using a limit entry order on a pin bar. Limit orders enable you to attract the market your way because you only enter a trade if it moves towards your preferred price. There are chances of missing out on the trade simply because the price may not necessary reach your preferred level. However, it is much better to use this approach because of the flexibility it offers.

2. Daily chart time frame: This chart time frame is a lot more relevant in setting out your entry points than you may be aware. This is because it is more useful than other charts with low time frames. The daily chart can be considered to be a natural filter for any bad entries. It actually filters out irrelevant and outstanding price movement of the lower time frame. Because of this, the daily chart signals become a lot more reliable.

Essential Tools for Market Entry

1. For the level pickers

Fibonacci retracement, trendline bounce, chart pattern bounce, bottom and top of range, the highs and lows, the top and bottom, and the Fibonacci target.

2. For the momentum breakout traders

Chart pattern breaks, break of the bottom or top, the trend line breaks, a fractal indicator break, and a break of the low or high.

3. For confirmation traders

Tools such as indicator confirmations, fractal break in anticipated direction, and candlestick formations in regions where support and resistance are expected.

Trade Style and Psychology

Generally, traders will have a preference of an entry strategy. This preference will depend on the trading psychology and style. There are traders who prefer to wait for a momentum break and cannot handle early entries. Others prefer to trade a pullback as these enable them to plan early. The trading psychology and style are crucial factors that often influence the entry strategy.

Stop Loss Strategies

It is almost impossible for any trader to survive the Forex markets without a reasonable risk management strategy. A stop loss strategy is one of the most important risk management strategies available to traders. Learning about the crucial stop loss strategies is absolutely essential.

The good news is that with stop loss orders, you will easily be able to protect your trades from negative emotions like fear and greed. If unchecked, such emotions can cause havoc to your trades.

What is a Stop Loss Order?

A stop loss order is simply any order that you place so that a security that you hold is sold when a certain price is achieved. The order is usually placed with your Forex broker. Such an order is created in order to minimize the losses a trader might incur after taking a position. It is absolutely imperative to institute stop loss orders any time a trade is initiated.

There are a couple of ways that such an order can be implemented. This is why it is important to actually come up with a good strategy that will suit a particular trade, market, or situation.

1. The Initial Stop Loss Placement

This particular stop loss strategy largely depends on the trading strategy that you choose. While there are some personal preferences that can come into play, it is one that is definitely common with many Forex traders.

If you adopt the pin bar trading strategy, then the stop loss can be placed directly behind the tail end of the pin bar. This move applied to both the bearish and bullish pin bars.

With the inside bar trading strategy, you should place the stop loss either behind the inside bar's low or high, or behind the mother bar's low or high. In both these cases, should the price hit the stop loss, they strategies become invalid and this simply means the set up was not sufficiently strong.

2. The Hands Off Stop Loss Strategy

Another excellent stop loss option that you can apply is the "Set and Forget" strategy which is also known as the "Hands Off" strategy. The aim of this strategy is very simple. As a trader simply set your stop loss strategy and just let the market run its course. It alleviates any chance of getting stopped way too soon as the stop loss is maintained at a relatively safe distance.

This strategy doesn't involve your hands so that you do not have to do anything once it is set up. The aim here is to ensure there is no temptation to make adjustments on the stop loss as you trade. There are some obvious advantages of using this particular method. These are listed below.

- Keeps emotional trading under control
- Eliminates the chance of getting stopped too early

- Frees up the trader so they focus on trades
- It is a very simple policy to implement

This kind of approach helps to reduce chances that a trade will be stopped too early by ensuring the stop loss is placed at a far enough distance. As traders, we know the challenges of moving the stop loss too early as our trades are stopped only to see the markets proceed in the correct direction.

It is imperative that emotions are eliminated from your trades. This way, reason will prevail and you will be successful in your trades thanks to this stop loss measure. All you do once you set up the stop loss is to simply sit back and let the market take its course. Also, this stop loss method is simple to implement because it is only handled once. Then as soon as it is set up, you can forget about it.

However, there are some disadvantages or downside of this particular set up measure. These are recounted below.

- Traders are often tempted to move the stop loss closer to entry point
- High risk because traders stand to lose the maximum possible amount

A trader who puts $500 on a trade stands to lose this amount as it is also the maximum possible amount that can be lost. This is risky and should therefore be approached with caution.

Sometimes traders feel the temptation to move the stop loss from where it is to where they feel safer. The Forex market is wrought with temptations and a disciplined trader should learn to fend off such temptations.

3. Break Even Stop Loss Measure

Yet another useful and applicable stop loss measure that we can institute is the break even strategy. Lessons on stop loss strategies are incomplete without this particular method. Traders often adopt this measure in order to protect their capital. Traders feel safe that they cannot lose money using this stop loss strategy.

Often, you will find traders moving their stop loss close to the entry price. This is not a bad strategy but at least it protects you as a trader. Here are some of the benefits of this strategy.

- You do not need to conduct market analysis with this strategy
- It is a very simple strategy to implement
- It gets rid of any imminent risk of a given trade

Once this strategy is in place, any risk to the trade is eliminated. Any market movements will then be protected by your stop loss measure, keeping you safe as the market plays out. Also, you will not need to conduct any complex, or simple, market analysis. Simply determine your entry point and use it to determine your stop loss.

The break even stop loss strategy is also one of the easiest strategies to implement. It is always easy to know where to place the stop loss no matter the trade. Even then, this measure has some disadvantages.

- This strategy hinders your odds
- It makes use of an arbitrary level which is not the best approach
- It puts traders at risk of emotional trading

Because the only determinant of the stop loss measure depends on your entry point and not market analysis, then this is an arbitrary approach. Such an approach does not portend much success compared to others.

This strategy will limit most likely limit your chances of success because it does not give any of your trades a chance to be successful. There is not enough room to move and maneuver. This is in contrast to the price action confluence that should essentially give you better odds. However, this stop loss strategy does allow the price action confluence to be in your favor and therefore affects your odds.

4. The 50% Stop Loss Strategy

This is a strategy that aims at cutting your risks by 50%. However, it does not necessarily cut your risks by exactly half. The main benefit of applying this strategy is that it makes use of the markets and enables traders to understand how much of their capital they need to protect.

Basically, if you apply this strategy and enter the market based on the daily close, the market may close slightly higher the following day. Now you can choose the day's low to determine your stop loss measure. Now, when the markets close the following day after your entry, you can use the low of that day to determine the stop loss point. This way, you will cut your risk by half. What this simply states is that should the market go below the previous day's low, then you will not proceed with the trade. There are some outright advantages of this kind of set up.

- Allows the use of the price action level
- Will cut your risk by up to 50%
- Gives your trades sufficient room to breathe

Cutting your risk by half is beneficial and actually good for your trades. For instance, if one of your trades was worth $100, then you could easily ensure that you lose no more than 50% on this trade.

This strategy makes use of the price action level. Due to this, it is unlikely that the market will get to the stop loss. In this instance, the market lows and highs are in play and hence the stop is protected. This is a much better approach as compared to other strategies such as the break even stop loss strategy.

Also this system allows the market space to breath. This means trades can freely occur without a trader having to exit. Market movements are essential if you are to make money trading Forex currencies. However, there are some downsides to this strategy. For instance;

- There is still the possibility of stopping trades prematurely
- Trades are still at 50% risk of loss

Although this strategy allows your trades to get some much needed breathing space, the trades are at risk of being stopped prematurely. This fact is particularly true for trades that involve currency pairs with volatile price action. Also, your trades will be at a 50% risk of losing out. This can be acceptable for some trades but unacceptable to others.

You can use market conditions during trade to determine whether the 50% stop loss strategy is the most suitable for your purpose. Take for example a situation where the market closed very close to the previous day's low. Then in such a situation, the 50% strategy would not work because it would have to be too close to the prevailing market rates.

Monitor your Stop Loss

When the market starts to move in a direction that favors you, then you should consider trailing your stop loss. Trailing the stop loss when the market is trending in your direction will help you protect your trading capital. It is important to note that a stop loss can be monitored either automatically or manually. Most modern trading platforms offer traders this option so they can choose if they wish to trail the stop loss or not.

The automated one is generally managed by the system so you will not necessarily need to worry about it. However, when manually following it, you will need to use price action levels in order to determine the trailing point of the stop loss.

Example

Take for example a trade situation where you purchase the Euro USD at 1.35. You can set the trailing stop loss at approximately 50 pips. Assume that the market actually moves in your favor and you gain up to 1.39 and this move gains you 400 pips. The stop loss will now adjust to 1.355.

It is therefore essential that you trail the stop loss marker manually, whenever possible, using indicators such as the price action levels. This way, you will remain safe and will use reliable indicators that give you more room to maneuver and allow trades to prosper.

It is absolutely critical that you use stop loss strategies as a Forex trader. There are a couple of strategies available so you will need to determine which is the most appropriate for each trade. For this, you will need to master how to use confluence to your advantage, how to use the best risk-reward ratio and how to define price action strategies and determining key levels.

Importance of Setting a Small Short Order

You need to set small short orders for a number of reasons. For starters, such short orders help to protect you from losses. This is essentially why it is so named. You trade to make money and not lose it. A small short order achieves this effectively.

The first and most important benefit of using a small short order is that it limits the losses to within acceptable margins. This is important because it protects your capital and limits exposure.

You can also effectively use it to lock in profits. This is why a short order is sometimes referred to as a trailing order. Locking in profits is crucial for Forex traders because profit is the main reason why we trade.

The short stop loss order also helps eliminate emotion from a trade. When feelings get involved and a trader uses emotions, then his trade will most likely fail and he will lose money.

There are some traders who do not use stop loss measures and instead allow a losing trade to run hoping the market will run and turn the trade around. This is a wrong approach that could cost you money and affect your trading capital. You should instead use a stop loss placement to mitigate losses.

Profit Taking Strategies

Every trader enters the Forex market in order to trade and realize a profit. All traders in the Forex markets have their own trading strategies. However, at the end of the trading day, they need to make money. It can be disastrous for a trader to spend precious hours trading the markets only to see their profits disappear simply because they did not know when and where to exit. Being able to identify the most appropriate exit points is crucial for successful trading on the Forex markets.

Even the best or most experienced traders need to have effective profit taking strategies otherwise they will lose money and become ineffective traders. Therefore, as a trader, once you are in a trade, your work is not yet done. Rather, it has only just begun. Trade management and exit plans need to be implemented and not overlooked. They are a huge part of trading but, sadly, are often overlooked by many traders. Most of the time the aim is to get out close to the top but actually the main objective is to make money. Here is a look at some of the most popular take profit strategies used by successful Forex traders.

Importance of Trade Exits

According to experts, trade management and exits are the most crucial factors of any Forex trade. They are even more important that the entry strategies. However, and surprisingly, not many traders pay attention to the management and exit strategies. Yet exits have the capacity to make or break a trade strategy.

According to research by trade experts and writers, no two traders approach trades the same way even under similar conditions. In most cases, the trader with the best trade management and exit skills will emerge the winner. Those without proper exit strategies may even incur losses.

Trade performance depends on a couple of factors that including trade management, limiting losses, and profit taking techniques. However, applying these techniques is not as easy as it sounds and many traders often fair poorly in this regard.

There are plenty of reasons why many trades are not profitable. Here is a look at some of these reasons.

- Watching a price move only to see it reverse direction before taking profits
- Exiting a position at an average price due to price retracement
- Traders sometimes move a stop loss and they opt to break even too soon

- Placing the take profit position close to the open price halfway in a trade
- Closing a trade too early and denying the take profit position to be attained
- Missing a market reversal and then losing all profits accrued

As traders, our instincts are always to grab a profit whenever the chance presents itself. This is natural and very common as we avoid losing the profit. However, this is never advisable. It is important to resist the temptation of taking profits early and learn to let the trade run its course. Delayed gratification in this case is way more profitable compared to instant gratification.

As a Forex trader, you really should learn patience and practice it as you trade. Also, you need to learn to stick to your original plan. All too often, traders change their minds and divert from the original plan. You will get much better results if you stick with the trade and initial plan.

1. Ensure that you Ride Winners Adequately

There is a saying about assurances in any trade. Basically, there are only two certainties that can occur. As a trader you will have winning trades and you will also have losing trades. To be a successful trader, you will have to learn to ride the winning trades adequately.

To be a successful trader, you should ensure that you fund your ongoing successful trades in order to make even larger profits. Let us assume that, as a trader, you have done your due diligence such as use technical analysis. If this analysis indicates that a winning trade still has some way to go, then you can pump in more funds into this trade so that you earn a much bigger profit.

Many professional traders say often that the success of their trades lies largely in riding on winning trades. There are a couple of ways to ride on a winning trade. One of the most popular ways of doing this is apply the pyramid process. This process simply means pouring in more money onto the winning trade with the hope of maximizing profits. Here is how the approach works.

- Let us assume the initial trade is allocated$15000
- The risk on this trade is put at $300

- A second position is then added as soon as the first gets to breakeven
- This second position should mirror the first one so add $15000
- This second trade rises and nears resistance
- You can have another pyramid at 60% so add $9000
- As soon as the resistance point is attained, take profit and exit

You will notice that you earn a lot more profit with this approach compared to letting it proceed to profit level. This is therefore an extremely useful tip that you can apply to earn significantly more money.

As you trade, there are some important aspects that you need to focus on. For instance, try and ensure that your stop loss' initial position is either at breakeven point or better. Ensure that the system where you are trading essentially has the potential to get the solid trending moves. But there is no need of using this approach if the risk-reward ratio is about 1:1.

2. Make Large Profits with Minimal Losses

The adage among traders is to let a winning run continue but exit any losing trades. However, applying this adage is not that easy for traders. This is because when faced with large profits, the instinct is often to lock them in. however, this is not the ideal approach of this particular strategy.

This strategy basically insinuates holding onto a winning position and hanging in there so the profits keep rising. Patience is a requirement for the success of this strategy. Anytime that a trade is heading your way and performing as well or better than expected, then profits will be on the rise. At such a time, you should not be packing and exiting the trade but rather hang in there, hold your nerve, and ensure you profit from the run as much as possible.

Like earlier pointed out, some of the wealthiest and most successful Forex traders are those who capitalized on profitable runs. A lot of the time, traders also need to learn to run away from losing trades. It is said that the first cut is the cheapest which loosely means that exiting a losing trade is beneficial if done quickly. The sooner you exit a losing trader the less money you lose. This will prevent you from suffering larger and more painful losses.

3. You can take your Money and Start Afresh

As a trader, you still have the option of exiting a trade and starting all over again. This strategy is more applicable to short-term active traders such as day traders. The main aim here is to collect sufficient profits from a successful trade within a certain period. Such a strategy does make sense especially to traders who wish to avoid taking risks with overnight trades.

Situations do change occasionally and overnight movements can wipe out any accrued profits. Taking profits within a trade and then closing the position and exiting the trade gives you a chance to start all over again and repeat the process. A lot of active day traders actively pursue this strategy.

There are ideally only two different ways of taking advantage of this profit taking Forex strategy. One is to apply a dollar or percentage profit target. Therefore, you can work out a suitable percentage for any given trade where you will take profits. As soon as the set percentage or dollar amount is attained, you should exit the trade and possibly start a new one. For instance, if you have a dollar amount target of about $500, you will trade until the amount is attained. Once attained, you should exit and then plan on the next trade.

Some traders use technical analysis to determine or guide their trades. Such traders often opt for technical profit levels. They often work with indicators such as the Fibonacci levels, support and resistance levels and so on. It is a great idea to consider using technical levels or indicators that can easily be used on any MT4 chart. This way, you will have an easy and clear indication about when to exit or stay in a trade.

Chapter 5: Top Options Trading Tools

Forex trader need access to a lot more information than what is generally provided through price charts. There are numerous tools they can use in order to trade prudently. The tools used are often referred to as technical analysis tools. These provide a lot of useful information that is essential for successful trading. The additional insights provided provide the necessary ingredients for success.

Technical tools are used in conjunction with chart overlays and statics. This will ensure Forex traders are able to make informed decisions as they trade. Some tools are suitable only for Forex trade while others are suitable for additional use like stock trading.

Trading platforms have what is known as a session highlighter. This feature is programmed to automatically display vertical lines across the price charts anytime that a major trading session closes or opens. Different trading sessions can easily be visually highlighted by the trader using a variety of colors.

Why Traders need Forex Trading Tools

Tools are absolutely indispensable when it comes to Forex trading. Fortunately most of these have become standard and numerous so brokers are able to provide their clients or traders on their platform some of the best tools in the market. A good example of a suitable trading tool is Meta Trader. Here are a couple of useful tools that you can use as you focus on your technique.

1. The Forex Calendar

You are likely to come across the Forex Calendar across different platform. Many brokers and traders provide this calendar on their platforms. Therefore, as a trader, you will most likely encounter this calendar when you enter the market. The Forex calendar contains a lot of information including economic news releases, fundamental events, and all current and previous values. Once information is released, the calendar is then updated so that the new information is also shared with traders.

One of the most common regular events displayed on the Forex calendar is the NFP or the non-farm payroll. The value of this figure changes on a monthly basis. This is why a lot of traders use this calendar as their primary tool when trading during such events.

2. Trading Terminal

Different Forex traders sometimes require different types of trading tools. For instance, if you are a trader observing multiple assets at the same time or a scalper, then the trading terminal is suitable for you. The trading terminal Forex tool enables you to buy and sell multiple currency pairs via the same window. As you trade multiple currencies, you will also be able to manage your trades and establish stop-losses as well as take profits whenever you have to. The terminal is great for multiple other things including numerous other Forex trading tools.

3. Mini terminal

This is a tool that is available with the trading terminal. Therefore, if you are keen on the latter then you should be able to handle the mini terminal. This is a pretty handy tool to have for any Forex trader because it supports Meta Trader's 1 click manager. Using this tool you will be able to do a lot all at once such as set your take-profit and stop-loss points with a single click. You can also purchase and sell Forex with one simple click of your mouse. This is a fantastic tool for most traders and especially day traders like scalpers and others.

4. MS Excel Forex Trader

Microsoft has developed Ms Excel Forex Trader which is an excellent option for Forex traders. A lot of experts in the field of finance use Excel for different applications and it serves them extremely well. As such it is a great idea to have it developed for various Forex applications.

You can easily connect Excel Forex Trader directly onto your trading platform. When you connect the two, you will receive currency pair prices directly onto your Excel. You will then be able to use any Excel functions and formulas so as to develop and analyze charts and obtain useful information for your trades.

5. Market Sentiment

This is an excellent Forex trading tool that especially useful for Forex positional traders. Using the Market Sentiment, you will be able to easily access a trader's true position all on a single dashboard. This tool also enables you to find out the number of traders holding long positions as well as those holding short positions.

Market Sentiment can help you determine whether you want to enter a trade and additional information such as your chances of success should you trade against the market.

6. Correlation matrix

Anytime that you examine a couple of Forex trading strategies you should try not to deal in currencies with correlation levels that are similar. The term correlation which it comes to Forex trading refers to the relation between the price changes of a currency compared to its pair.

A correlation matrix enables traders to gain insights into currency pairs correlations that are mapped out over different time frames. This is an amazing tool especially for novice traders and beginners in general because it enables you to avoid putting your margins in currencies that should be perform in a similar manner.

Forex trading tools summary

The notifications provided by the various Forex trading tools may not necessarily free but are crucial for the success of your trading strategy. They provide important data and information that is essential for implementing a successful strategy.

For instance, you will be notified if the stop-loss level or take-profit level is attained. The notifications provided by Forex tools are important for numerous traders especially those who may not be in possession of charts when they are needed. There are plenty of other tools available. They serve different purposes and are applied whenever a situation demands it.

More about Forex Trading Tools

Forex volatility tool:

This is a trading tool used by Forex traders and indicates the movement of a currency pair. Sometimes traders may be interested in the average movement over a period of thirty days. The volatility tool can narrow down the results to a brief period of the day. The information is sufficient to let you know how volatile a currency pair was during a certain period or day of the week and how the volatility changed with time. Volatility tools do not indicate the direction that a trade is heading but can inform a trader the magnitude of price movement.

Forex position summary tools

As a trader, you can sometimes receive an updated summary of your positions from your broker. This summary basically lets you know the position of other traders in the market. You can receive a summary showing 40% of clients are long on the USD/EUR while 60% are short on the same pair. This information on its own is not really helpful. What is more important is the change with time of the ratios. When the price moves, it will be possible to get deep insights on future price movements.

There are some tools that provide both historical position rations as well as currency position schools. These are extremely important if you wish to view the position ratios have indicated price direction change. For example, a price reversal can be deduced should current positions close in on historic levels.

Technical Indicators

Forex traders have a wide choice of tools to choose for their trading charts. These technical indicators include moving averages, RSI and even the MACD. Other less common ones include the TTM Trend, the envelopes, and the zigzag.

It is possible to customize the zigzag so that it indicates the percentage movement of the price and this can point to market tendencies of the price action. For instance, zigzag retracements often indicate that currencies basically retrace close to 56% of a trend then pulling back before proceeding in the same direction. Such a pattern can easily be picked out by a trader who will then fine tune the location and timing until a proper entry and exit point is identified.

Envelopes generally consist of three parallel lines that appear just above the price action. The line in the middle is the moving average. The envelope is generally used to provide an outlook on the possible trend direction and changes and also whether we have a weak or strong trend. If the price touches the top of the three lines then this means the trend is headed upwards. We can also adjust the moving average so that it behaves as either resistance or support.

We also have the TTM Trend which is a useful technical indicator. It tends to change the price bar colors on the chart. The changes in color will depend on the direction of the short term momentum. The bars will turn to a blue color when the trend heads upwards and red when the trend begins a downward movement.

In summary, technical indicators are not just the major ones like the moving averages. They are simply tools that can provide traders with information from other sources of information such as statistics and price formations. They can be used in combination to make them more effective. Remember that you do not have to use all these indicators when trading. Simply practice using a demo platform how to use them and then find the ones that work best for you.

Chapter 6: Preparations Prior to Market Entry

Building a trading plan is by far the single most important aspect of your success as a Forex trader. You absolutely have to take time and plan your trades from start to conclusion. All too often traders will enter a trade without a clear plan or vision. They believe that a particular trade is a winning one and they fear losing out. Such traders jump into a trade and start making profit. However, once the tide turns, they turn around and try again. This will lead to huge losses and profitability might be missed simply because there was no pre-trade planning.

It is crucial that you treat trading as a business and not a side gig or hobby. This way, you will take it more seriously and will have a better chance of success. If you have no idea what a trading plan or how it looks like, then it is better to learn as it is among the most crucial aspect of your trading life and success.

Forex Trading Considerations

As a trader, you need to understand that the key to success is actually emotional discipline and not intelligence. If the main ingredient was intelligence, then there would be a lot more people out there trading and making money. Even before you begin trading, think about the reasons why you are a Forex trader? What are your desires, ambitions, or aspirations? Are you seeking financial freedom or to be your own boss? Do you want to establish an additional source of income? Once you answer these questions, then you will be able to determine your motivation. It is this motivation that will keep you going from day to day, month to month and even for years to come. You need to keep in mind that trading Forex can be a fulltime job and is never a gamble. You can actually make money.

Have Realistic Trading Goals

As a trader, you need to think realistically about your goals and how you will go about achieving them. For instance, you cannot, as a trader, expect to earn a living trading Forex with an initial of $50, $500, or even $2000. With goals that are realistic, you will be able to set targets and meet them, feel motivated and keep going. Realistic goals also enable you to abide by risk management and money management rules.

Here are some realistic goals that you can set for yourself.

- Always have a trade strategy
- Trade according to your strategy
- Be consistently profitable after 12 months
- Ensure capital growth by 3% each month

What type of trader are you?

You need to determine what type of trader you are. There are different kinds of Forex traders. The type of trader you aspire to be is mostly related to your persona as well as the time you have to dedicate to your trades. Forex trading essentially occurs in timeframes. You need to determine the trading timeframe that suits you best. Here is a look at the different types of traders.

1. Scalper:

A scalper is basically a trader who prefers trading the lowest timeframes. Such traders do not want to wait for long hours for their trades. They enjoy speedy setups and enjoy a lot of time with the charts each day. A scalper searches for the lowest spreads within a currency pairs and often opts for the business times of the day for any major Forex currency pairs.

2. Day Trader

Most Forex traders are day traders. And many aspiring traders often envision themselves as day traders. Such traders don't enjoy scalping and they consider it to be nerve wracking. They are also not happy leaving trades open for lengthy periods of time. Day traders have plenty of time in their hands throughout the day and can spare moments to find trade setups and keep observing and monitoring them throughout the day. A day job is basically

3. Position Trader

A position trader is a Forex trader that enters a trade then finds and holds a position for a long while. This could be for weeks at a time and sometimes even for months. Therefore, they always base their trades, decisions, and moves on the fundamentals of a currency rather than technical analysis like other traders do. Such a trader needs to be very patient and must be able to predict the activity of the market within a month or longer. Such traders work with large stop losses mostly because of big market swings. They also need substantial capital amounts to affect their trades.

4. Swing Traders

A swing trader is a Forex trader who is happy to leave his or her trades open for a couple of days. Such a trader generally follows market swings in the correct direction. Swing trades often plan their trades intricately and prefer to focus on only a couple of trades at a time. These particular types of trades are suitable for people who do not have much time for their trades but are patient and willing to wait for lengthy periods of time for their trades to work right. Patience is a virtue for swing traders so keep that in mind. They also need to be disciplined enough not to exit a trade should the market move against them. An impatient trader would feel compelled to intervene, stop a trade, and possibly start a new one.

Determine the Kind of Trader you are

Part of your trading plan needs to contain your preferred type of Forex trade. When you eventually make the decision, make sure to write it down as part of your larger trading plan. There are a couple of things that will basically determine the kind of trader you are going to eventually become. These include your trading strategy.

Ideally, your trading strategy should define a couple of things including how you plan, select, open, manage, and eventually exit a trade. It is very likely that you have an idea on how you accomplish each step but it needs to be written down as part of your strategy. For instance, how do you choose your trades? What are the determining factors or essential ingredients?

Here are some of the essential ingredients that constitute a good trading strategy.

- Do you have a trading setup? Your trading setup should include things such as technical and fundamental indicators as well as trading timeframe.
- Do you have any established rules?
- Are there any exit tools?
- How are stop loss and take profit strategies determined?
- Will you use a trailing stop?
- Are there conditions that would compel you to quit a trade early?

What about Risk Management?

One of the most essential aspects of Forex trade and trading in general is risk management. This refers to the percentage of your trading capital that you are willing to risk in any trade. It also points to the risk: reward ratio. As a trader, you may be wondering how much of your capital you should be willing to risk. The answer basically should be not more than 2%. Therefore, anytime you want to come up with a trading strategy, always think about risk management. Risk management is always considered using the risk: reward ratio or the 2% maximum risk allowed.

Always Keep a Trading Journal

Another important aspect of trade planning is keeping or maintaining a trade journal. A trading journal is simply a logbook where you record all your trades. You should endeavor to make this as routine as possible. This is an excellent way of turning you into a profitable trader within a very short period. A journal allows you to take and record notes so that you note what great things happen and any lessons that need to be learned. It is important to keep a trading journal because;

- It allows you to record notes of your emotions and sentiments while trading. For instance, if you thought you were losing but ended up winning then you should not this down.
- A journal provides a reliable record of all your activity. This historic record enables you to conduct an analysis of previous trades so that you can determine what you did well and where you went wrong.
- It also enables you to confirm whether or not you followed the trading strategy that you had set out for yourself. If there were any discrepancies or failures, then these will become visible to you.

Summary of a Good Trading Plan

Here is a summary of the proper steps you need to take to come up with a suitable trading plan.

- Take into consideration your motivation for Forex trade

- Work within realistic goals so that you attain them
- Discover the kind of trader that you are
- Use a template to write down your trading plan
- Always have a risk management plan
- Ensure that you keep a trading journal

How to Make a Reliable Trading Plan

We have already determined that a Forex trading plan is essential for a successful trading strategy. Any plan that you come up with should be written in stone which means it should not change. However, it can be subjected to a review once the trading day is over or after the market has closed. Your plan can be adjusted as market conditions change and changed as your skills get better. Avoid using someone else's plan and come up with your own.

Asses your skill set

You need to determine whether you are ready to trade or not. If you have a system then you should test it until you have confidence that it works. You need to be like the professionals who trade the markets confidently. They move in and take profits from traders who have no plans and keep making expensive errors.

Have a check list and a routine

Any good trading plan should consist of a routine in trading activities. It is important to have a pre-determined routine so that you do not end up running around confused and out of focus. With the routine you will also need discipline. Also, you should choose the most obvious market setups whenever you can so that you pick up any easy trades. You can in fact formulate your entire trading plan and make it a check list. Having a smooth format that enables you to determine if a trade setup is worth it is absolutely important.

Trade Preparation

Make sure that you carefully determine the program and trading system that you will use. If you intend to use signals, then ensure that these are easily visible and can be detected clearly with a clear auditory or visual signal.

Come up with clear exit rules

A lot of traders often focus more on finding buy signals. 90% of their attention is spent looking for entry points and so on. However, they pay very little attention to the appropriate points of exit. Often, traders will not sell when they are down as they are unwilling to take a loss. To make it as a successful trader, you will need to overcome such concerns. A lot of professional traders lose more trades than they win but because of their money management and exit rules, they still end up making a profit.

Therefore, always find out your exit points before you enter a trade. Each trade has at least two exit points. Write down your stop loss points and do not count on mental notes. Also, ensure that each trade has a profit target. Once you hit this target you should collect some of your profits and then move your stop loss position to break even. Also, do not risk losing more than the percentage that you initially set.

Prepare yourself mentally

It is extremely important that you prepare yourself for the day ahead. You will need a clear head and focus. A good trader always has to be up to the challenge. Experienced traders will tell you that it is better to take the day off and not trade at all if you are psychologically and emotionally unprepared. Otherwise you will simply not be able to participate fully in any trade and you will not only lose huge amounts of money but will worsen your mental situation.

It is easy to be mentally unprepared when you are angry, distracted, or preoccupied with other thoughts. As a trader, you may want to have a mantra that you repeat regularly, probably once each day. Such a mantra should put you mentally at ease and into the trading zone. Also, avoid distractions within your trading area. Trading is business and distractions can cost you in a huge way.

Do both your homework and due diligence

It is important that every morning, just before your trades begin, you should become acquainted with the goings on around the world. What is the situation at the markets? Are overseas markets up or down? Is there any company about to release its earnings report? Most traders prefer to wait for the release of such reports before making any major moves. This is a much better approach than taking unnecessary risks. You can use index futures to gauge the mood of the market right before the markets open.

Come up with clear entry rules

Just like with the exit, you need to define and set clear entry rules. These rules will define how you enter a particular trade. It could be something like; if I have a signal B which fires and indicators show minimum target about 3 times larger than the stop loss and I am at support, then purchase Y contracts or X shares.

The system you use needs to be sufficiently complex to handle instructions effectively yet flexible enough to manage any snap decisions. For instance, if you have a total of 15 conditions that need to be fulfilled while most are subjective, then it may be challenging if not impossible to actually trade. It is worth noting that computers make much better traders compared to humans.

This is probably the reason why half of all trades on the New York Stock Exchange are executed by computer software and not people. Computers carry no emotions when trading. They simply follow a program set by a trader. When conditions are met, then they enter a trade. Should the trade proceed in the wrong direction, then they exit. But should a trade become profitable then the computer will take profits and exit. All decisions are based on probabilities and devoid of emotions and irrational thinking.

Post trade post-mortem

It is advisable to conduct a post-mortem of each trade. While adding up the profits and working out any losses is important, understanding why is ten times more important. Have a trading journal where you write all your conclusions so that you learn, improve, and remember.

Summary

It is important to gain sufficient skill before embarking on Forex trading. There is never a guarantee that any trade will make money. However, your chances as a trader will improve drastically if you are sufficiently skilled and have a system that can assist you win. All professional traders choose trades where the odds favor them otherwise they wouldn't trade. However, during trades, they allow their profits to ride a winning trade and cut their losses short. This can result in some losses but they will emerge winners overall.

Many traders who do not make money often do not trade the way that the pros do but instead do the exact opposite. Learning and improving skills should be one of your hallmarks. Also, as a trader, you need to treat your Forex trading as a fulltime job, part time job, or a business. It is never a gamble or a game where you depend on luck. This way, you will take is seriously enough and aim to make rather than lose money. While no trade is ever guaranteed, it is crucial that you have a suitable plan so that you have much better chances of winning and making a consistent profit.

Chapter 7: Forex Trading, Charts and Practice

There are several ways for Forex traders to enter the market. These include quantitative analysis, fundamental analysis as well as technical analysis. All the methods help Forex traders determine the direction or movement of Forex currencies.

Some traders may choose to use direct information such as events in the news, policies, economic variables, government policies, and things of that nature. Others prefer to use Forex trading charts together with other indicators. These, when used in combination, provide sufficient information that can guide a Forex trader to make appropriate decisions.

Regardless of your preferred trading method, you will actually need to learn how to read Forex charts. It is best to have a good grasp of the basics as well so that you eventually become a great Forex trader. Basically, you must learn how to crawl before you can walk.

What is a Forex chart?

A Forex chart is simply a chart that contains historical information on currency exchange rates. Using these charts, a trader will obtain information that they need to conduct technical analysis in relation to a specific currency pair. In short, a Forex chart is a graphical representation of the exchange rate between two currencies.

You are likely to come across Forex charts on most Forex platforms provided by respective brokers. Brokers often provide these to clients who have open and funded accounts.

If you examine a Forex chart closely, you will observe how the exchange rate of a particular currency pair has been changing over a period of time. The reason why these charts are important is because past financial events are great indicators of future events. Financial instruments such as currencies have been known to follow similar cycles and paths throughout history.

Forex chart timeframes

The amount of time indicated on a Forex chart depends on the exact timeframe that you want. Most of them however are set based on the one day timeframe by default. Therefore, a single point on the chart represents a single day's trading information. This is not fixed and can be changed to provide whatever timeframe you prefer.

Technical analysis

The information obtained from the charts will be used for technical analysis. The term technical analysis simply means reviewing past market analysis and prices with the use of technical indicators in order to foretell the future. Technical analysis helps foretell future market events and short-term movements.

According to Forex traders, price movements in the short term are caused by demand and supply forces. When charting in order to predict future price movement, you will need to use charting software. You will also need to choose from numerous technical indicators such as moving averages and so on. As a new trader, you should try out a couple of brokers to find out what their charts offer before choosing one.

Type of Forex charts

There are a couple of Forex chart types. The most common are the bar chart, line chart and candlestick chart. Most traders prefer the candlestick and there is a reason why. Candlestick charts contain a lot more information compared to the line and bar charts. This information is actually four times that produced by the line and bar graphs. It includes low and high prices, as well as closing and opening prices. This extra information gives you the advantage of knowing the price movement over a given period of time.

Forex indicators

We use currency charts to enables to better study and analyze market behavior and also determine currency movement for the future. For this to be implemented successfully, traders need to use additional indicators. There are numerous such indicators available. Most Forex traders use only some of the most crucial ones. These are mentioned below.

1. *Bollinger bands:* These are volatility lines that are located or aligned next to moving averages.

2. *RSI – Relative Strength Index:* This is a momentum indicator and shows the velocity and direction of price movements.

3. *SMA – Simple Moving Average:* This is one of the most popular indicators used by Forex traders. Together with other moving averages, they are mostly used to level out fluctuations in price over a specific period in time. They provide traders with a better visualization in regards to the price movement and direction.

Practice before Live Trading

It is extremely important that you learn how to use the Forex trading platform and how to make use of all the features available. The good news is that most brokers and all other platforms do provide demo accounts. Using these demo accounts, you can invest virtual money then apply a trading strategy and see how well you can implement one. Having the ability to test your skills and try out different strategies is an excellent way to get started. Once you get an understanding of how Forex works, you will simply need to open a demo account and begin implementing different strategies. With time, you will eventually learn how to trade Forex, how to interpret and apply your analysis and so much more.

Most major brokers provide customers and potential clients with a free demo platform that they can download and use. This is recommended before any client begins trading because familiarity with a platform makes trading easier. There are certain things that you should be on the lookout for even as you learn how to trade and apply different strategies.

Paper Trading

The term paper trading originated from the stock markets. Years ago, some traders wanted to practice trading before eventually trading live. These traders would take pieces of paper and then follow the market movements as they practiced trading.

Markets attract new traders all the time. Many of them are wary about losing their money and hesitant about entering the market directly. Many would rather learn the ropes first, practice trading, and once they feel confident enough, they'd enter the market. Paper trading is a common form of practice prior to entering the markets.

Trading has some level of risk involved. This is why it is important that you learn how to trade in order not to lose money. Different platforms provide different tools to their clients. These include demo platforms for practice. Paper trading is not as popular today as it used to be before. Since things went digital some years back, paper trading is sometimes referred to as trading a demo account.

Through the years, stock markets and Forex markets have let novice traders and beginners trade on their markets without actually putting any money at risk. As such, traders can enter trades confidently and practice their trading skills. They get opportunities to try out their skills and test their strategies. These are awesome cost free opportunities to try out different strategies and find out the ones that work best.

Modern and advanced technologies allow investors and traders to practice from any location they may be and at the time of their choosing. As such, traders gain useful opportunities to work on their skills and implement strategies so they know how different strategies perform when implemented under different market conditions. Such traders gain a unique advantage over other traders elsewhere because of the chance to paper trade.

Paper trading on the digital platform also enables traders to become fully conversant of different parameters and features available to them. They are also able to easily and freely navigate across trading platforms with ease. Today's trading platforms are versatile and robust and come with numerous tools and different features. Gaining as much experience as possible using these features and tools is crucial for successful trading on the markets eventually.

Benefits of paper trading

There are some obvious benefits of paper trading for all traders but especially novice traders and beginners. One of the top advantages of paper trading is that traders are able to trade without risking any capital. The thought of trading without risks enables traders, especially beginners, to gain sufficient practice and hone their skills.

More experienced traders also use paper trading when trying out new channels or testing a new strategy. By using paper trading, they are able to try out these new strategies and channels without worrying about losing money. Traders also get to learn the Forex market much better and gain a better understanding the kind of trader that they are. Paper trading therefore plays a useful role in the world of Forex trading.

Today paper trading is accomplished digitally. This means that traders have to open digital accounts and trade using a digital demo account. A demo account receives virtual money which can be spent trading on the virtual platform. All you will have to do is implement a particular strategy by opening positions and funding them. Demo accounts operate exactly like real Forex accounts including the features that they come with. In essence, traders at all levels get to enjoy stress free trading on a platform that is very similar to the real one.

Users of demo accounts they also have the benefit of learning from their mistakes. We all make mistakes and learning from them is the best that we can do. Therefore, demo accounts which are modern day paper traders are important in a number of ways. However, there are a couple of disadvantages.

Disadvantages of paper trading

There are some downsides to paper trading. One of these is euphoric trading. Since there are no losses to incur traders can get careless and trade without a care. Traders end up taking major risks with their trades since there is no money at risk. In reality, traders never make highly risky trades for fear of incurring major losses. Paper trading causes traders to lower their guard and risk most of their funds.

Money lost on the demo platform is inconsequential and never taken too seriously. This is a major challenge because it introduces complacency. Traders tend to place trades on their demo accounts that they wouldn't dare on the real platform using real money.

Also, funds are crucial when it comes to Forex traders. We need to be careful with our trading capital at all times. Unfortunately, demo platforms or paper trading cause us to be careless and traders may end up losing large sums on the live platform if they are not careful. Some traders also fail to act as thought the market was a real one. This way, they will not always follow the markets and their trading approach may be affected.

In some instanced, demo accounts experience delayed data. Basically the data available is never actually fresh but old and outdated. Some platforms use fake data while others introduce delays. The main aim of paper trading is to sharpen a trader's skills and prepare them for the real platform. Fake or delayed data does not strongly support this aim. Traders sometimes refer to paper trading as "Trading with paper money or monopoly money". This creates an attitude that belittles trading altogether.

Is paper trading worth your time?

According to experts, paper trading is definitely recommended. It provides an excellent platform for traders to hone their skills and practice trading without worrying about incurring losses. However, traders should treat paper trading with the seriousness it deserves.

If done well and taken seriously, then paper trading will enable traders to try out their strategies, make use of different features and come up with the best strategy possible. Practice definitely makes perfect so novice traders who spend a lot of time paper trading will improve their skills, understand the workings and functions of the trading platform and much more.

Also, a trading simulator is the most suitable trading tool that learners need. Such a platform will help to transform them from amateur traders and novices into profitable traders in just a couple of weeks. You also get to learn your level of risk, things such as trading discipline, and the type of trader that you are. Therefore, when the opportunity of trading risk-free on a demo platform arises, you should seize it and practice as often as possible. This way, you will eventually become an excellent trader who is consistently profitable.

Forex Trading Platforms

There are plenty of Forex trading platforms out there. Most of these have plenty of similar features and even appearance. There are some common ones that you are likely to come across. These platforms include the MT4 and MT5 which are abbreviations for Meta Trade 4 and Meta Trade 5. These two are currently the most popular. Some traders do not offer demo platforms at all. You have to sign up and open an account in order to access one.

Platforms are generally different but most of the functions available are pretty similar across the board. The most common features are technical analysis tools, charts, drawing tools, news feed, Forex quotes, trade history as well as buttons that enable purchase and sale of stocks.

There are platforms that have a lot more features than your average broker provides. You are likely to come across certain economic and fundamental analysis tools which are not found on other platforms. These are extremely useful to traders seeking long-term ventures. However, short-term traders can thrive without these additional tools.

On the trading platform you are also likely to come across shortcut features that help to save you time as you execute trades. You will also notice additional features such as buttons that provide access to information on current trades, latest news, and so much more.

Place virtual or demo orders

Now that you have a better understanding about Forex trading platforms, it is now time to place your first order. Experts advise beginners and novice traders to place at least 50 different trades on a platform just to gain the necessary experience. This way, you will be sure that you have sufficient trading experience in order to go live and trade using real money. Before you trade live, there are a couple of questions that you should ask yourself. These questions include;

- Do I know how to set up a stop order?
- What is the procedure of setting up a limit order?

- Is it possible to have a stop order and limit order for the same trade?
- How large are the lot sizes that I can trade? (e.g. 1,000 units)
- Is it possible to mix and match different lot sizes?
- Am I able to phone the deal room should my internet slow down?

You should be able to answer all the above questions before trading using real money. Otherwise you will probably be risking your money because your skills may not be up to par.

When you want to purchase a currency pair, you need to get to the chart and click directly on the prices. To purchase Forex pairs, you will view some quotes featuring your preferred currency pair. There is the ask portion of the order and the bid part. You should click on the ask part of you wish to purchase and bid if you wish to sell.

There are platforms that let you select the limit order or market order once the quote window appears. Some others make it mandatory to make a choice beforehand. Once you decide on the currency pair and price, you should then choose volumes. This simply means the quantity of trades you wish to enter. Once the volume is determined, you should determine and enter both the stop-loss level as well as the profit-take level. These are the points during trading where you exit once you start taking losses and where you collect profits and exit a trade respectively.

You will notice that there are different kinds of orders such as pending orders and market orders. Should you want to purchase or sell at indicated price levels, then you should select the market price. If you wish to sell or buy at different price levels then choose the pending level. Once you have filled out the form completely, you should submit it. This will complete the order placing process and the order will be received.

Treat the demo like real trading

Once you begin trading on the demo account, you should first focus on mastering the different functions and other trading basics. Checkout your different strategies and implement them one by one as best as you can. This way, you will be able to identify the one that you like best.

There are different kinds of strategies including long-term trading with less leverage, short-term momentum traders, scrappers, day traders, and so on. It is only through practice that you will be able to find the ideal strategy for you. Even then, demo trading is simply Forex trading practice and not actual trading. You should apply yourself to these demo trades the best way you can. This means treating trades with seriousness and care.

Sometimes you may incur huge losses on your demo trades. You may not feel anything and will simply remain calm because you haven't actually lost anything. However, in real life, even small losses may jolt you awake. If you want to benefit from demo Forex trading, then you should treat the trading process as if it were real. As an example, you should trade with $5,000 and not $50,000 if you intend to fund your real account with only $5,000.

Prepare to Enter the Forex Market
Chapter 8: Essential Preparations for Live Trading

Forex traders, especially beginners, need to learn about the steps necessary for profitable trading. Achieving long term success trading profitably is a dream that many have but only a few can achieve. Fortunately there are steps that you can take that will ensure you become a successful, long term, profitable trader. Here is a look at some of the essential steps that will lead you to successful trades.

1. Choose the Right Broker

When you feel totally ready to begin trading Forex currencies, then you should first embark on identifying a fair, trustworthy, and reliable Forex broker. You may be a great trader but without a reliable and trustworthy broker, you will not be as successful as you should.

You may have an idea of what a Forex broker is but it is important that we define who he is so that you have no doubt. A Forex broker can be defined as a company or firm that provides traders like you with access to a trading platform. As a trader, you need this platform so as to gain direct access to the Forex Market. Brokers are usually compensated via the bid-ask spreads of a given Forex currency pair.

The first step you should take is search for reviews of the broker and find out what other traders think about him, his platform and services. Conducting due diligence is a must for any serious trader. You also need to check out the trading platform to find out if it matches your needs. Different traders have different needs when it comes to Forex trading so finding a right match is crucial.

Most Forex brokers will allow traders, who are possible clients, a chance to try out their platforms and test their services. They do this by offering a demo account. This provides traders with an excellent opportunity to try and understand how the system is like, how it functions and operates. As a trader, you need to try out as many platforms as possible so that you find one that you are quite happy and content with.

The Forex market operates 24 hours a day and sees a daily turnover in excess of $4 trillion. This makes it the world's largest financial market. as a trader, you will need some help navigating this market so your broker should be able to assist you as you trade on their platform.

1. *Check for regulatory compliance*

Most reputable Forex brokers are members of the NFA or National Futures Association and also registered with the US government as a commission merchant via the US Commodity Futures Trading Commission.

The NFA is an industry-wide body and self-regulating organization that covers the entire futures market in the USA. On the other hand, the CTFC is an independent government body that regulates the options markets and commodities futures markets in America. Their aim is basically to protect the public as well as market users from manipulation.

A professionally looking website belonging to a Forex trader does not in any way guarantee that the broker is registered or regulated. Most of them will state that they are registered with the authorities and will display their registration details. You should never deposit your precious trading capital onto just any trading platform. Deal only with Forex brokers that are properly licensed and duly registered.

2. Apply Proper Customer Service

Traders can access Forex markets at any time of day or night because the markets are accessible 24-

hours each day. Your chosen broker should be available to provide you with essential services all the time. It should also be pretty simple to be able to access someone on phone for help. While chat-based service will do most of the time, there are instances when speaking to a real person will be of great assistance. Before signing up to any platform, consider making a quick call to customer service just so you get a feel of the quality of the customer service that they offer.

3. Study the Currency Pairs Available

There are plenty of different currency pairs and even individual currencies out there. However, when it comes to Forex trading, only a couple of pairs are of any major importance. Some of the most useful Forex pairs include EUR/USD, GBP/USD, USD/CHF, and USD/JPY. Some top Forex brokers might offer a wider choice that may include the Chinese Yuan, the Hong Kong dollar, Australian dollar and so on. Always check out the list and ensure that the currency pairs you are interested in are available.

4. Take a Closer look at the Trading Portal

As a trader, you are connected directly to the Forex markets via the portal. It is therefore absolutely imperative that the portal is visually presentable and simple to use. You will be using this platform to practically carry out all the operations of your trades. Ensuring that it is in excellent working condition, easy to use, and reliable is something you must do. A good trading platform should come with essential buttons such as a simple sell or buy button. It should also come with an emergency button that allows traders to close all their open positions.

If the platform is poorly designed, then it will put your trades at huge risks. For instance, you could go short instead of long, or accidentally add to a given position instead of closing, and so on. Such mistakes will not only cost you money but also emotionally distressing. There are excellent options out there such as the Meta Trader which is among the most popular options among Forex traders.

While there is no perfect Forex broker in the world, identifying an excellent platform will allow you to focus more on your trades and technical analysis. You will then have more time to focus on developing appropriate trade strategies.

The Essential Features of Online Forex Brokers

Every major Forex broker offers accounts with various features. These include some of the following.

1. Leverage and margin

As a trader, you will have access to a wide range of leverage amounts. These amounts will really depend on your Forex broker. Leverage could be 50:1, 100:1 and so on. The term leverage simply refers to a loan that you can access if you are a margin account holder. If you are an account holder and your account has a capital of $1000, then a Forex broker offering leverage of 50:1 will allow you to hold a position worth $50,000.

Leverage does work in favor of a trader especially when holding a winning position. The reason is that such a position stands a great chance of being profitable and making money. However, caution is needed because if a trade starts heading in the wrong direction, then the potential for losses is huge and could wipe out a trader's account. Therefore, caution is imperative whenever leverage is sought.

2. Spreads and Commissions

Online Forex brokers make their money mostly from spreads and commissions. Some opt for commissions which charge traders a certain percentage for accessing their platform. Sometimes the broker will charge based on the difference between the bid and ask price of a currency pair. Most traders prefer not to charge a commission but instead prefer to charge or make a commission from spreads. Generally it is harder for a trader to make a profit on a wider spread. Common trading Forex pairs like the EUR/USD or GBP/USD have much tighter spreads compared to other pairs that may not be as tightly paired.

Forex brokers often offer first time traders or new clients a free amount which they can access and use to trade. Most Forex accounts are funded with very little money, sometimes as little as $50 or $100. However, this amount can greatly increase due to the offers and access to leverage power. This is among the reasons why Forex trading is so popular with first time traders. As a new trader with a new account, you will have the option of opening either a mini, standard, or micro account. Each account has a minimum deposit requirement so this is worth noting.

3. Ease of withdrawals and deposit

Generally all major Forex brokers have their own policies when it comes to depositing and withdrawing your money. They also have things such as a funding policy and so on. A good broker will enable a variety of payment options including use of credit cards, direct payments from bank accounts or ACH, use of bank checks, wire transfers and also use of online payment processors like PayPal and others.

Withdrawals from accounts are often processed via wire transfers or checks. Reputable brokers usually charge a processing fee during withdrawals. However, there is often no charge for making a deposit. You should check out these features before signing up with any broker.

Learn Proper Money Management Strategies

As a Forex trader, you will have to take risks with your capital. There is no strategy that is 100% profitable and even professional Forex traders lose money on some trades. The focus is always on the amount or percentage lost. Before entering any trade, you need to have a good strategy including the loss you are willing to incur before exiting a trade.

Most traders are willing to risk between 1% and 2% of their capital. Some are willing to get to 5%. However, the percentage you choose will largely depend on your risk appetite. There are a couple of things that you need to keep in mind though. When trading, the volumes could increase drastically and this could have an effect on your capital. You will need to be flexible with some of your money management techniques when the time calls for it. This way, you will avoid losing money on your trades.

Some of the essential money management techniques that apply here include setting up your stop loss strategy. You need to decide exactly where to locate this important feature. The stop loss feature can be adjusted based on the current situation in the market as well as its volatility. It is only after the stop loss process is complete that you will decide on the volumes of trade. Remember that money management is a crucial step and decisive part of any profitable trading strategy and should, therefore, not be overlooked but treated with the seriousness that it deserves.

Have the Right Trading Psychology

A successful trader has many admirable characteristics. These include the ability to determine stocks' direction and understanding a company's fundamentals. However, the single most crucial characteristic is the ability to exercise discipline and contain emotion.

What is Trading psychology?

One of the most significant aspects of trading is the psychological aspect. Traders are often jumping in and out of trades on very short notices. Most of the time traders have to make very quick decisions with immense ramifications. A certain degree of calmness and presence of mind is therefore required. Emotions should never be allowed to cloud a trader's judgment or cause them to deviate from established trading plans.

The area of Forex trading is quite high paced with numerous possibilities and just as many pitfalls. Most of the time traders feel like the odds are stacked against them. Anytime a trader receives news about a certain currency, it is not uncommon to get scared. Sometimes they overreact and feel compelled to end a trade and other irrational acts. By so doing, a Forex trader may prevent losses but will also lose out on any possible profits.

Understanding fear

Traders need to understand what fear. This is a natural reaction to what a person perceives as a threat. Traders need to face up to this fear and see how they can get rid of it. Conquering fear is never easy and it does take some time and practice but it is an essential aspect that needs to be tackled sooner rather than later. It is important for traders to isolate the single fear element, focus on it and try to isolate it as they trade. This is not as easy as it sounds but it works eventually.

Greed is your Worst Enemy

On Wall Street, traders have an adage that says, "Pigs get slaughtered". This saying simply means that any greedy Forex traders will eventually lose out. Such traders tend to cling to a winning position and try to earn as much money out of it as possible.

Overcoming this negative emotion is never easy. This is because greed is based on a positive instinct that you can do better. However, getting just a little more out of a trade can cause a lot of trouble. This is why it is advisable to learn to keep emotions in check, to have a suitable trading plan and to determine the profitability and any losses on any given trade.

Tips and Advice for Successful Forex Trading

Trading is more of an art than a science even though it is known for its ratios, charts, graphs, and numbers. Therefore, apart from learning the theory, you will need to hone your trading skills through regular practice and discipline. Keep doing self analysis and test your trading plans to see how effective they are. There are essentially a number of steps which, if adhered to, will ensure that you trade safely and also make great profits.

A lot of undisciplined and inexperienced traders have incurred large losses over the years. You do not want to be like them. If you can determine the important steps and tips that will keep you safe and earn you money, then you will definitely be successful.

Never 100% Successful

It is a fact that no trader is ever successful 100% of the time. Many lose some of their trades but then they win big on other trades. Successful Forex trading is possible and can happen. However, you should not expect a 100% win rate. As a trader, you should endeavor to match up to the behavior and personality of the Forex markets. This means you should align your thoughts and practices to align with the Forex market and how it works and not the other way around. This is an absolutely crucial point. You should NOT endeavor to bend the market so it becomes what you want it to be.

You can Succeed with 60% Wins or Lose with 80% Wins

Winning up to 80% of the trades you enter is absolutely phenomenal. A 0.8 win ratio is very respectable in the Forex world. However, you still lost

20% of the trades you entered which can be a little disappointing. Yet there are traders and trading systems that experience 60% wins or less. It is possible to be successful with only 45% wins.

Take the example of a trader who invests $1000 with the chance of winning $5000. Such a trader can afford to lose 4 trades because with just one win, he will emerge $1000 richer. This is how it is possible to emerge a winner with less than 50% wins.

On the other hand, consider the trader who invests $5000 to win only $1000. This is a risky set up and the trader cannot afford to lose. The losses will be too costly. While this is just a demonstration, it shows how it is possible to lose over 50% of your trades and still emerge a winner.

Reduce your Overall Risk during Trading

There are plenty of factors that determine the outcome of a trade. As your skill level increases so will your ability to spot lucrative trade setups. Trading can be simple but is never easy. As a trader you should endeavor to reduce your risks and exposure when trading in the foreign exchange markets. Here are some steps that you can take in order to keep yourself and your trades secure.

- **Start Trading with Small Amounts and Increase Organically**

One of the best tips that you can use is to start small. Do not load your account with a huge sum but try and start small. Use small amounts and low leverage. This is very important. You will be able to apply the skills you have learnt and focus on trades without the fear of making huge losses. If you are to grow your account, then ensure that you grow your capital amount organically. This means let the capital grow from the returns of your trades and not loading your account from other sources.

- **Timing is Key so learn to be Patient**

As a trader, you really need to learn patience because it is an essential ingredient for success. One of the most important acts should be your opening trade. This is a crucial trade so you should give it your best analysis. You should also assess all other potential trades in good time. Make sure that you correctly time your market entry because correct timing for this initial entry is crucial for success. For this you will need to apply all your skills and knowledge about market trends and charting techniques. You should also ensure that you understand the entire process so that you are absolutely sure of what you are doing.

- **Learn the Limits of a Position before Entering**

Every time you enter a trade, you must not only set your stop loss but also determine the maximum allowable loss that you are willing to take. The rules are pretty simple: Make sure you only risk money that you can afford o lose. Also, ensure that anytime you assess a position size and money required, there are sufficient funds for the trade. Avoid mixing cash meant for other projects with your trading capital.

You also need to set a total loss limit at the close of each month. If at any one time during the month you get to this limit, then trading should cease and you should wait for the following month. Also, should your losses consistently exceed your income, then you should probably cease trading and take a step back. Take time to reassess your strategies, revamp your technical skills, and trading fundamentals. Also, have a journal of all your trades so that you review them and take note of where it is that you are going wrong. Should you go back to trading and start making profits, put aside some funds just incase anything goes wrong. Such setbacks should be mitigated with the funds you set aside.

- **Remember to be Diligent and with your Trading Plan**

As a Forex trader, you will enjoy success when you eventually learn to balance hard work such as chart analysis with sound judgments and lots of patience. Too many traders often give up on their trades without giving them sufficient time to run their course. This is why a majority of first time traders and investors eventually give up and quit. To be a winner, you should learn patience, stick to your plan and do not quit.

How to determine the most Suitable Trading Strategy

There are many Forex traders out there who spend years implementing trading strategies that do not match them. This can be disastrous because the chances of success are very low. It is important to make some considerations before embarking on trading using a particular strategy. Here are some useful points that you should consider. When you take these points into consideration, then you are likely to save yourself a lot of hurt, pain, time, effort, and money.

1. Determine if you Want a Regular Income or Grow Wealth

First let us understand the difference between earning an income from trade and growing wealth. If you trade Forex to earn an income, then you probably target to earn a certain amount each month for your own personal use. However, when you want to grow wealth, you aim to grow your amount by a certain percentage each year.

Trading for an income

If you want to trade Forex in order to earn a monthly or weekly income, then you need to identify trades that occur within a short period of time. It also means that you should spend more hours on the trading platform. Some of the options you have regarding trade strategies include short term swing trading, day trading, and scalping.

Trading to grow wealth

You can choose to have fewer trading options when you want to grow your wealth. This essentially allows you to spend fewer hours on the trading platform by choosing trades with higher timeframes. Some of the trading options you can choose include position trading and swing trading.

2. Determine the Amount of Time you have

You need to decide how much time you can dedicate to Forex trading each day and each week. People with a fulltime job and those who cannot put in 12-hour days should consider Forex strategies that do not require a lot of time investment. These including position trading and swing trading.

Forex trade strategies like scalping, day trading and all other short term trading strategies are for traders with all the time in the world. Therefore, choose any of these strategies if you enjoy them.

3. Find out if a Particular Strategy Suits you

There are a good number of Forex trading strategies out there. All these can be split into two distinct categories. These are high win strategies with low reward: risk ratios and the low win rate with high reward: risk ratio.

You need to determine which of these two approaches suits you best. Apparently, they can both make you money as they are both profitable. Therefore, you need to determine which of these two categories you are more comfortable with.

Do you wish to take huge risks for high returns or are you comfortable playing it safe with low risk trades? Swing trading, for instance, has a high chance for success but with low returns. On the other hand, position trading has lower win rates with much larger gains.

Summary

In short therefore, we can conclude the following:

Swing trading: This strategy can be used for wealth creation or income generation. It is suitable for traders who can only spare a couple of hours each day to trade.

Day trading: This strategy is more popular with traders seeking to generate a regular income. It requires a Forex trader who has time on their hands and can spend long stretches of time in front of a screen.

Position trading: This is more of a wealth building strategy and is best suited for traders who do not have a lot of time on their hands. Such people often have another job or occupation elsewhere.

Before you embark on learning about any of these Forex trading strategies, you should first make the following determinations.

- What trading goals do you have?
- How much time do you have available?
- Does a particular strategy or approach suit your personality?

Only when you are able to address these concerns should you then proceed to start trading.

Conclusion

Thank for making it through to the end of this book, let's hope it was informative and able to provide you with all of the tools you need to achieve your goals whatever they may be.

The next step is to begin practicing the various skills and techniques you have learnt. Remember that trading is not theoretical but practical. As such, you need to get onto a platform and begin applying your knowledge. No Forex trader has ever enjoyed success by simply reading Forex topics widely. Gaining knowledge and information is advisable and you should do that. However, of greater importance is applying this knowledge, honing your trading skills, learning the ropes, and simply becoming a better trader each and every day.

As a rule of thumb, you should not begin trading until you have a clear understanding of how Forex trading works. There are lots of important things involved including technical and fundamental analysis, reading charts and interpreting the direction and all the various strategies. Only after plenty of practice over a number of weeks should you then begin to trade. When you feel ready and comfortable on the trading platform, then you can place your first trade and see how it goes.

Remember that there is a lot that makes a great trader. For instance, you need to be disciplined and have your emotions in check. These are essential ingredients for success. Basically, if you apply all the things expressed in this book, then you should become a successful Forex trader in time.

Finally, if you found this book useful in anyway, a review on Amazon is always appreciated!

www.ingramcontent.com/pod-product-compliance
Lightning Source LLC
Chambersburg PA
CBHW060827170526
45158CB00001B/98